T0164892

SLEEPING TO AWAKE

NATALIE NOKOMIS

BALBOA.
PRESS

A DIVISION OF HAY HOUSE

Balboa Press books may be ordered through booksellers or by contacting:

Balboa Press
A Division of Hay House
1663 Liberty Drive
Bloomington, IN 47403
www.balboapress.com
1 (877) 407-4847

Printed in the United States of America.

ISBN: 978-1-4525-9743-0 (sc)
ISBN: 978-1-4525-9744-7 (e)

Balboa Press rev. date: 10/20/2014

CONTENTS

CHAPTER 1

KNOW HOW TO USE IT

I have always suspected that I should write a book. There have been quite a few people along the way who have encouraged me to do the same. The events, people and places that I have come to find as "normal" have been deemed not so normal from others who have known me. I guess I wouldn't know since all I know is my life.

I grew up feeling different from the masses, as I'm sure many of us do. I wasn't going to work a nine to five in a cubicle, get married, have kids, go to college, or have any sort of traditional life at all. There is nothing wrong with people who have these types of lives, it just wasn't for me. I always knew that I was born unconventional and ardently curious. I have a strong propensity to question just about everything; mostly myself.

I have discovered that everyone is an artist in some shape or form. We are all painting a huge canvas called LIFE. We are designing, creating, molding, and shaping daily, unbeknownst to quite a few of us.

It seems that most of the people I have attracted on my path have been like-minded while others have been on the complete opposite end of the spectrum. There have been artists, musicians, gypsies, hippies, alcoholics, and some very bohemian type folks with some of the most interesting and strange beliefs and worldviews. I have also spent my fair share of time with ordinary people who turned out to be just as ordinary as they seemed. I have learned many valuable life lessons from some of these folks, while others have had me discover precisely who I DO NOT want to be in my life. I believe that sometimes we can learn from people more about who we do not want to be than who we do want to be.

The most memorable quote I have ever heard still remains with me after twelve years. The quote came from a drunk and foul smelling homeless man on the blue line in Chicago. He was in a frenzy pacing back and forth. His hair was all dreaded, matted and harboring who knows what in between the strands. As the train would come to a stop, people would enter and he would sit down next to them looking all kinds of crazy. Suddenly, he would compose himself and momentarily transform into a Sunday morning Gospel Preacher declaring, "KnowLEDGE is power, WISdom is knowing how to use it!!!" (I deeply wish I could convey to you his boisterous tone and animated mannerisms through written words.) I'm sure this quote came from some philosophical mind of the twentieth century and was by no means of his own making. I found it quite insightful and amusing that he was completely owning it and saying it with such persuasion. You could see the hamsters in people's minds starting to speed up on the wheel a little bit. I mean the fact that this guy was clearly not following his own advice and decreeing it with so much conviction got me thinking....

It reminded me of me. I will be the first one to pull out a quote for just about any occasion. You name the life event, I've got a quote. My old standby is, "Everything happens for a reason." It's appropriate for every circumstance and I believe it to be true. This saying brings light to a situation and may have people momentarily believing in some sort of divine plan. Most of the time, however, it leaves them wanting to slap me for being so cliché and persistently optimistic.

When I heard this man speaking his abandoned truths, I no longer wanted to talk the talk; I wanted to walk the walk. What would it look like if I actually took all those quotes, theories, ideas and beliefs I ramble off frequently? What if I was infused with infectious positivity and genuinely knew that my life is always on the right path? What if I knew that everything that happens to me in my life is for me to evolve to a higher level? What if I could inspire people to get these truths for themselves? I mean I have an arsenal of knowledge, what would happen if I actually opened it up and let it explode into the world? What If I was wise!?

This book is about my life. The way it has been, the way it is and the way it will be. These are the situations and events that have shaped and transformed my points of view and perspectives on just about everything. When I learned that the way to change the world was by starting with myself; I hated the idea. I mean clearly it was everyone else that was unconscious and ignorant, not me. These are just a few of the stories of how I went from being a self- loathing, angry and suppressed girl to becoming a confident, clear headed, and in love with myself woman. Everything in life is truly an opportunity to learn something you did not know before. It is an occasion to grow; experience and prosper. Most of all it is a challenge to turn the unforeseen into an opening for awareness, expansion and action. We are not stuck or doomed no matter what the circumstance. We were meant to flourish, blossom and cultivate that which is innately in us. It wasn't an easy road and it never is. I am clear there are many others who have had it light years worse than me, however we ALL have the power to shift our conditioning and beliefs about ourselves, people and the world if we open ourselves up, peek inside and learn to ride the wave of life instead of swimming against it.

CHAPTER 2

APPARENTLY, I TALK TOO MUCH

I don't think we ever quite understand the impact our kindergarten, grade school and high school teachers have on us until we are old enough to question it. I'm sure college professors and teachers do as well. I wouldn't know because I didn't make it that far.

I spent Kindergarten through eighth grade in Catholic school. I loved having choices being made for me and being conditioned to believe things I couldn't even comprehend at the time. All in all it was my Grandmas idea to make me go and who can blame her? Public schools are frightening, especially in the suburbs. The city may be scary but suburban kids are scarier. They may have metal detectors and the occasional altercation in city schools but they have bored, spoiled and emotionally neglected kids with way too much money in the suburbs. That's a scary mix.

I puked on the American Flag when we were saying the Pledge of Allegiance, I think that was the moment I decided I was different. Sister Mary Ann was not pleased, but remained a bundle of joy while folding up the flag and placing it in the trash can.

I was practically raised by nuns, priests and religious types. When I started looking at myself and the ideas I have about myself, the first place I started was with my teachers. I learned quite a bit from some but there were a few rotten eggs that really make my blood simmer when I think about them. It is not because I believe their assertions about me. It is the fact that I now have to un-condition my conditioning and that's hard work.

Sister Mary Ann, my Kindergarten teacher was sweeter than molasses and had more energy than a qi gong seminar. She told my Mother I was such a precious child. She also said I was very outgoing and that I loved to talk. Even though I threw up on her American flag, this woman loved me unconditionally and believed that I was an angel. Needless to say, I liked her very much.

First through Third grade are quite a blur. I can't even remember my first grade teacher. My Mom chose to move to the city with her new husband and take me along for the ride. My first day of school I recognized that my skin wasn't quite as dark as everyone else's. Furthermore, the teachers weren't anywhere near as nurturing as they had been in the suburbs. I didn't dislike it but I really didn't like it much either. I don't really have all that many memories of it besides tucking my skirt into my tights when I was in the locker and everyone laughing at me as I walked out. I didn't know why they were laughing but figured out that my butt had been sticking out as I strolled coolly across the classroom. This is probably the moment I became forever embarrassed of my body.

I have no memory of my teacher but do recall a boy I had a huge crush on, his name was Joey. Every day at lunch I would give him my Twinkies or whatever other fun thing my Mom would put in my lunchbox. Our last names were very similar, so naturally I was convinced he was going to be my husband. All I would have to do is add a letter to my name. Needless to say, things didn't work out with Joey and when the year was over my Grandma and Uncle rescued me from the city and brought me back to the sleepy town suburbs.

Second and Third grade are really not that notable either. I know I had nuns for teachers for both grades. My third grade teacher looked older than Petra (if you don't get the reference, please look it up) and she reminded me of a skeleton. I can only remember the way she looked not how or what she taught. What I remember for sure is that in both grades when they had parent teacher conference night they would tell my Mom and Grandma that I talked too much and I really needed to learn to pay attention and focus in class. It was affecting my grades. I apparently had good social skills but was taking it a little too far in their opinions.

Fourth grade was the beginning of my real issue. My teacher hated me for some reason and to this day I don't know if she really did or if I was making it up. Ms. Sarpetto was the spitting image of an overweight evil sea witch. She was the epitome of a woman miserable with herself. She was rude and condescending and even told me I was stupid. She told kids to shut up and would take her frustrations out on all of us. She picked and chose the kids she was decent with and was cruel to all the rest.

At that point I really started realizing that I was different and thinking she was jealous of me and all my classmates. I'm not sure why I thought that but I did. She would actually call my house and tell my Mom and Grandma that I misbehaved in class and distracted other students. Me!? A distraction!? The nerve!!

My art teacher had to of been the worst of these cast of characters. She was very gifted and artistic, however did not try to nurture or grow the students who weren't so naturally artistic. There were a few students that were very talented and would get to do cool projects, receive special treatment and her full attention. I have zero ability to draw or paint. I can do abstract stuff but when it comes to drawing things from physical reality...forget it. She was not a kind person in my opinion and would make the kids that weren't gifted clean up after the other kids. She wouldn't let us participate and told us that we were untalented and incompetent. I remember her energy vividly. She would complain to my family members that I talked too much too, what a surprise.

I'd really love to know what I was always talking about so much? I really liked myself and how friendly I was. I loved being with other kids and playing and just having fun. I remember these times as being uncensored.

As time went on and I got into junior high and high school my suppression button got turned on permanently. Situations past told me I should not talk so much, I was stupid, untalented and unartistic. I was told that I am the opposite of everything I really am which is fabulous with social skills, intelligent, and more creative than an alliterated hip hop verse. Thank God my eighth grade teacher who was open minded and played guitar wrote me a letter before I went off to high school and told me I should and would be an amazing writer.

I absorbed a lot about life from these past situations and personalities. The main thing I learned is to only believe the wonderful things people say about you. They are complimenting and praising you for a reason and if they didn't really mean it, they wouldn't say it. Question those people who tell you are less than and make you want to turn your suppression button on. Don't believe the negative things people say about you because a lot of the time they wish they could be more like you. When people speak about you either in front of your face or behind your back in a destructive and unproductive way it only means that they are unhappy with themselves. Always remember who you are and don't base your opinion of yourself on someone else's interpretation or perception because most of the time, they're wrong.

CHAPTER 3

DIFFERENT BEATS

In grammar school, I had a crush on a red headed boy named Steve. My obsession with "finding the one" started in Kindergarten. It all starts so early, our search for love, romance and acceptance. The educators of my school would write on my progress reports that I needed to be quiet and not be so sociable as I said before. This was funny to me because I always thought I was an introvert. Most of the time I was inside my head, judging everyone, and wishing I was someone else. In the background, however, I always secretly adored who I was. It would take my whole life to finally understand this.

There were only 26 people in my graduating class and about seven of them were the meanest little bitches you ever did see. They formed a secret group called, "The Meow Club" of which I was not allowed in. I never understood why people didn't like me. I was so harmless and fun. I later came to discover that when you march to the beat of a different drummer sometimes you get excluded. When you are authentic and call it like you see it most people don't respond well because quite a few of those people are living lies and following the masses. Truth in the face of deceit is a very confronting thing. Also, it's mostly those people that you are jealous of that are jealous of you. It's nothing but a mirror. Who knows what the truth is?

I remember the first time I learned what sex actually was. The leader of the "Meow Club" described what she believed it was. She told us the man takes his thing and puts it inside of the woman. I was forever scared. For one because I wondered what a "thing" was? That made no sense to me and as you'll find out later I stayed scared......real scared. These girls just walked around and did whatever they wanted. They were all rich and lived in big houses and would get to go on space camp trips and do typical suburban kid stuff. I always felt out of place, which is probably why I moved back to the city at 17. I didn't belong with all those stuffy, snobby brats

When I would get on the bus in the morning some kids would make fun of me. Trees would hit the window and make a funny noise and all the kids would say, "Natalie farted." They would ask me why my family was so weird. "Why doesn't your Mother live with you?", "Why does your Grandma wear all that makeup?," "Do you have a Father? Where is he?" and so on. They would chant derogatory things and call me fat. I always thought everyone was so much better, prettier and smarter than me. They would all amount to something and me to nothing. I was a mediocre nobody.

I isolated myself sometimes to the point of being a hermit crab. I would sit in a tree in the backyard and think about why we're all here, the meaning of life and existence and fantasize about numerous different scenarios for the way my life should have turned out and the family members I wish I had. Why was I an only child? Why didn't I have a Father? Why didn't I at least know who my Father was? Why didn't my Mom love me enough to actually live with us? Why was my life situation so different than everyone else's I knew?

When you have a unique and non-conventional life situation, sometimes people will shun you. Conformity is the comfort zone for most of us human beings and stepping outside of that can lead to quite the discomfort. It's no surprise that conform and comfort are very similar words. Marching to the beat of your own drummer can leave other people paralyzed and spiteful. Us own drummer types end up hating ourselves and thinking we are "weird" when in reality we are the ones that actually have the courage to grow. We are the ones that actually bring a heartbeat and life to life. We are the ones that have the audacity to have real conversations with people and not just speak of superficial things like sports and weather. Most people are their own drummers, they're just too afraid to grab their drumsticks. Many of us are terrified of being ourselves, and where does that get us? It has us experience ourselves as fake and leads to unhappiness and dissatisfaction. What fun is that? Us own drummer types are the ones that actually take the lives we have been given and create what is beautiful and true for us and we leave behind the need to be accepted. We desert that there is one cookie cutter correct way to live life. There will always be people who disagree with your philosophies and your lifestyle choices, however it is up to you whether you are controlled by it or not. Is it really other people who are oppressing you or is it actually you?

CHAPTER 4

THE GREEN MAN

When I was about five or six years old I was sleeping in my Mom's bedroom in our house on Elmwood where I grew up. It was a big red ranch house with huge picture frame windows that seemed to go from the floor to the ceiling. The house was a one level and had four bedrooms. My Moms and my room were on one side of the house while my Grandma's and Uncle's were on the other.

For one reason or another I had always felt a little creeped out in that house. Maybe it was the spaciousness of it. It was pretty cluttered but there was still an airiness about it that not too many other houses I had seen had. It had an attic and a basement, neither of which I really ever went into. The story went that some depressed lady had hung herself in the closet of my Moms room just before they had purchased the house. If it would have been me purchasing the house this would have been a deal breaker but I guess certain things only bother certain people. I can't remember one night where I didn't sleep with the blanket over my head. I remember always thinking something was under the bed or in the closet, of course this could have been due to watching incessant episodes of "Tales From The Dark side" and "The Twilight Zone." All I know for sure is that I knew something was in that house. There was just something different, eerie and weird feeling.

I woke up sometime between two and three in the morning, I can't recall exactly. I walked to the opposite side of the house to the kitchen to get a glass of water and ran back through the house as I always did, scared that something would follow me or jump out at me. I thought something was going to get me. The so called "house settling" as my grandma always called it sounded like voices to me a lot of the time.

I returned to my Moms room with a glass of water in hand, drank it and then popped back into bed with her. When I got under the sheets and was settling in I looked out the door of her room where a heating vent was located. I stared into the darkness as I saw a long stream of green smoke being expelled from the vent. I stared and stared and all of a sudden the smoke looking substance turned into a physical form. I was paralyzed with fear and felt like I couldn't even breathe.

The figure became more and more clear and turned into a grim reaper looking type thing. It was kneeling on the floor with a black cloak over its head. It had a rosary held in between its green hands and slowly cocked his head forward. I was staring and in complete and utter disbelief. As it slowly turned its head up to look straight forward I saw that it had a gooey slimy green face and red eyes. It was straight out of a horror movie. I kept on telling myself that I was seeing things. I kept saying," it's just a dream, it's just a dream" and realizing that I was wide awake and this was no dream. This was real. I shook my head and then turned back and it was still there. I closed my eyes for seconds at a time only to reopen them and find it was still there. No matter what I tried it didn't go away. At this point, while still staring at this monster I can only describe as a green man I started hitting my Mother begging and pleading for her to wake up. She wouldn't budge. In her half sleep stupor she just kept saying, "go back to sleep." By this time I had taken my eyes off the door and the green entity had disappeared. I laid still, staring out the door for hours waiting for it to make a re-appearance and it never did.

I believe this is the moment I shut down my ESP. I know I had abilities as a child but they were not embraced or encouraged so they got put on the backburner of my mind. I view this as a time when I wasn't understood and decided it would be better to just act as "normal" as though nothing had ever happened. It was quite interesting to me considering that my Mother was an artist and had painted a spaceship she said she had seen when she was in her early twenties. Maybe she knew something about me or us that she didn't want to deal with or couldn't explain well enough to be understood. What I know for sure is that we are all highly perceptive and attuned to energy even though a lot of us don't have awareness about it. I believe we are all highly intuitive and that we need to reclaim that gift and birthright. We have gotten so immersed in the physical world that we have completely taken our energy and focus off that which really matters. We truly are spiritual beings having a human experience and once the masses realize this and we deconstruct religion the world will thrive in harmony and love. It's happening more and more, however media and fear propaganda have us believe that it is not. They have us focus on things of the physical world and create reality TV shows that are the furthest from reality you can get. They feed us garbage and we eat it. Who are "they?" I do not know, but I do know we are being controlled without even knowing it and we have to take our power back. Those of us who do know about it, which is quite a few, need to start speaking up and coming forward for the sake of the collective consciousness. Einstein said, "The world will not be destroyed by those who do evil, but by those who watch them without doing anything." The easiest way to do that is to eliminate all negative forces and influences from your life. You don't need to go out and start an orphanage or create some elaborate organization to eliminate poverty in foreign countries. If you want to that's fabulous, however the most powerful thing we can do on the planet right now is take responsibility for ourselves and our actions. We can quit playing the blame game and ask ourselves, "What can I do to make a change?" We have to return to our sanity and sacredness. We have to respect and adore each other and ourselves. If it doesn't make you feel good, do not engage. If you watch a TV show and find yourself comparing yourself to everyone on it, turn it off. If you listen to a song that says horrible derogatory things about woman, turn it off. If you eat fast food every day and you feel lethargic and disgusting after eating it, stop eating it. It's time to raise the vibration in every possible way and the only way to start is to live in love. First and foremost you must love yourself. Eat healthy food, listen to empowering music, watch movies that are uplifting and only hang out with family and friends who are empowered and want to move forward in life instead of dwelling on the past. Don't let other people steal your sunshine and brilliance. Focus on love, freedom and light. We are divine creatures who can create a sustainable, harmonious and utopian planet. Start with you right now.

CHAPTER 5

NEVER TRUST A CARSALESMAN

Even though I was only four years old, I remember that phone call. It was early in the morning and I answered. I had been sleeping in bed with my Mother, who was living with us at that time and rolled over to pick it up. A deep voice spoke on the other end and requested talking to her. Little did I know that it was a man my Mother had met the previous night while working her last shift before quitting the local diner she worked at. In retrospect, I didn't know how significant that phone call would be to her life but it indeed was the start of a tumultuous, abusive and obsessive relationship.

Jon was his name and he was one of the angriest and saddest men I had ever met, which is basically the same thing. It's funny the things you realize once you've grown up that you had no clue about and took as normal when you were a child. There are so many things I remember about him and an equal number of things I choose not to remember.

I remember the way he smelled of some type of low quality cologne and that he would always wear the same blue velour shirt. Most of all, I remember him insulting and cutting my Mother down quite consistently. He was a loud and angry man with an unquenchable thirst for destruction.

Jon had two children from a previous marriage and their names were Tessa and Taylor. Even at that age those names highly annoyed me. I mean do people really have to name their kids so matchingly? Both of them were dirty blond and petite. They had shiny sparkly hair, got really tan in the summer and were both way more beautiful than me I suspected. They would wear cute little bikinis in the summertime and when their Mother would dress them she would make sure they had the latest trends and stylish haircuts. I never felt important when they were around. I would see them mostly on the weekends. One time they showed up and had chopped all their hair off to be replaced by super chic 1980s cuts. That week my Mom made me chop all my hair off to match. I hated it. I always felt like I was the odd one out and that I was somehow strange or weird. I didn't want to be like them and felt like my Mom was just trying to make me fit in with them. Instead it made me resent them more.

Looking back I now know that Jon had some major mental issues he hadn't dealt with, after all his Father was an alcoholic that used to physically abuse him so how could he have not adopted those same habits? It's seems that we either copy what we see when we're growing up or we go the total opposite direction and route, there doesn't seem to be an in between.

Jon had a black and white tuxedo style cat that he put in the microwave one time. I remember watching the cat spin around inside and it felt like the longest twenty seconds of my life. I was so young and utterly confused as to how and why someone would ever do such a thing.

There was one time in particular that I'll never forget. We were standing in the kitchen and my Mom was making dinner. The kitchen table they had in their house was the same one that he had been in his parent's house when he was growing up. He grabbed my head and shoved my face sideways cheek down on the middle of the table and held it firmly there. He pretended he was punching and hitting me and told me, "This is what my Father used to do to me when I was a kid, I would get the shit beat out of me" This was quite disturbing to me but I was ecstatic that I wasn't getting smacked for real. My Mom just stood there in disbelief. She looked shaken and docile at the same time.

When I was about ten I had gone back to living with my Grandma and Uncle due to how strange the relationship between Jon and my Mother had become. My Grandma and Uncle and other family members were not too fond of him given the stories my Mom would tell them.

One rainy night, my Mom showed up to our house with bruises and blood all over her. We took her to the hospital and they admitted her in to the psychiatric ward. Seeing my Mother in that state at that age devastated me. I loved her so much and couldn't believe that anyone would be capable of doing that to such a beautiful woman.

I visited her in the mental ward and she had made me some handmade moccasins. The patients there were encouraged to do creative things to take their minds off their minds I suppose. I recall when she handed me those moccasins I realized what a brilliantly gifted artist she was. I thought, "No one else's Mom would be able to design cool shoes like this, what an awesome Mom I have." This obviously made me even sadder. I sat down beside her bed and asked her why she was still with Jon. I had begged her to leave multiple times to no avail. She told me she loved him and didn't want to leave him. I felt like he trumped me. She was more concerned with preserving her relationship with him than raising and being there for me. Jon knew it too. He knew he could do no wrong in her eyes. He knew that she would never leave him no matter how bad he treated her. He was a manipulative liar and a car sales man (I know not ALL car salesman are bad guys, but quite a few in my experience) if that says anything, a true professional bull shitter.

Jon was definitely a lesson in learning who I did not want to be in my lifetime, he was truly a man who was repressed and had not let go of his past. He didn't know any better than to mimic what he had been taught and what he had seen and known growing up. This is pretty typical of most of us. We tend to not question why we are certain ways and why we do the things we do. For many of us it simply seems too hard and for others we succumb to a state of laziness or complacency. We just take who we believe ourselves to be as the truth and believe ourselves to be stuck in certain patterns. We feel trapped and immovable at times, like it is impossible to modify our behavior and break through our repetitive ways. Jon learned to be angry, bitter and jealous and never figured out that he was not condemned to being that person. He never figured out that he was responsible for his life and existence, not his alcoholic Father.

CHAPTER 6

THANKS MOM

I'll never forget that phone call. The one that told me I needed to get on a plane as fast I could because my Mom probably wouldn't make it through the night.

I was sixteen years old, pubescent, and miserable. I spent most of my days thinking about what my purpose on this earth was, not giving a shit, thinking everything was a joke and contemplating why everyone else was stupid and I was different. I couldn't quite figure out why I didn't fit in anywhere and why there were a select few people who found me to be interesting.

My Grandma and Uncle raised me from the time I can remember. My Mom was always in and out of the picture due to her hopeless romanticism. I can remember at least five men at random times in my very early life. They always seemed to be tall, dark handsome and foreign. She had a thing for Mexicans, or maybe they had a thing for her? It was my understanding that if you big hips and an even bigger ass most Hispanic and Black men will be interested in you. I mean really though you won't be able to make in through a construction site or a family diner without getting a creepy unnerving look or at least a few hisses. Anyway, my Mom always had some type of man around and ended up settling for the worst one who I've already talked about.

Most of my childhood was spent trying to figure out why my Mom wasn't around that much. My Grandma became like my Mother. She was the one that eventually took me to school, fed me (too much), and watched Friday night sitcoms with me. T.G.I.F was my favorite, especially "Family Matters" because it took place in Chicago. My Mom would either be working at one of the many diners she was employed at, which probably was in an excess of twenty throughout the course of her life.

I never understood it. My Mother was an artist and very attractive. She had green eyes that looked like a cat and one dimple when she smiled. She was so beautiful and eccentric. She had a vast array of knowledge and I always felt that she was connected to a higher power. It seemed that she had something blocking her from completely connecting. I always felt like she was so intelligent but was not practicing what she was preaching. She was not demonstrating the progressive ideas that she acquired from the many books she read. If you tried to give her a compliment she would never take it. She always seemed to be broke and dating a guy that wasn't anywhere near the plane of existence she was on.

My Mom would tell me the coolest stories about her life. She told me she saw a UFO in our front yard one night when she was coming home from work. There were actually burn marks on the ground. She painted pictures of mystical things like wizards and goddesses. She had a bohemian spirit and a heart filled with too much love, so much that some people would take advantage of her unbeknownst to her. She never saw her own beauty, creativity or talent but we all did.

My Mother was an amazing woman who also passed on her insecurities to me. She had obviously learned them from my Grandma who had learned them from her Mom and so on. There was always just a feeling of self-loathing and hatred that permeated her space. It always seemed like there was drama and a lot of crying. She wasn't physically well seeing as though she was diagnosed with juvenile diabetes at the age of three. She didn't take care of herself like she could of, another surefire sign that she just didn't care about herself. I learned that if you are not respecting your body, mind and spirit through nutrition, exercise and spiritual well-being you are not aligned with the vibration of love.

I know she loved me with all her heart, how could she not? I was her only child. A fatherless child, a child that she didn't believe she could take care of due to her lack of self-love. I suspect that's why she left me with my Grandma and Uncle a lot. She ended up living in California and Nevada for a few years and I would go visit over the summer. Being 16 in Vegas really wasn't all that much fun but I would make up lies and elaborate stories of the interesting people I met and share them with my friends when I got home.

When I received that phone call that hot day in June it was a life shattering moment. I knew that my Mom had been sick in Vegas, she had just separated from Jon finally and was on dialysis a couple times a week and on a kidney transplant list. The thought of her not being with me in this earthly existence tore me up inside. I called my Uncle at work and he rushed home and booked our flights for the following morning. I still to this day don't know where he found the money for that.

We arrived in the dry, stifling air of Las Vegas that morning and headed to the hospital she was at. I just remember the whole thing being completely surreal. I couldn't believe that this woman I loved so dearly wasn't going to be here with me anymore. Even though we were two thousand miles apart she was always in my heart, always with me even though not physically. I would talk to her almost every day on the phone and she would always send me fun things in the mail, sometimes even a check for 100 bucks. I would feel guilty for taking it considering I knew she worked her ass off at the truck stop to make that money.

When I walked into the hospital room the reality hit and it hit really hard. She had already started losing her color and turning a faint shade of cyan. She was on life support and the doctor told us we had to make a choice of whether to keep her alive or not. At this point she was clinically brain dead and pretty much a vegetable. I held her hand and it felt so cold, it felt like death was in the room, chilly and empty. In moments of experiencing someone dying you either turn to or away from a higher power. I chose to turn towards. The doctor escorted us out of the hospital room into a little side room which seemed to be where all the hospitals staff received their mail. As the doctor was talking to me I turned my head and the first mailbox I caught sight of said J. Christensen and all I could think of was how interesting that that's what it said. It was like Jesus Christ.

Now I am not religious by any means, although I did go to Catholic school for ten years, it felt more like brainwashing to me though. Christianity and Catholicism did not resonate with me when I was a child and got even further away from me when I got older. I do currently believe it is a path for people to follow and fully respect that however it is not mine at this point in my life. I have a view that there are certain physical beings that walked this planet that knew things that no one else knew and were ostracized for it. If you look in history books or do any research whatsoever you'll find countless examples throughout the course of time. I imagine that there were ascended masters, people who were more evolved than this plane could handle. In that moment looking over at that mailbox I knew that my mom was ready to go. She had done what she came to do on this planet (although to me at the time it appeared she had not done much.) In retrospect, I know she fulfilled her purpose. She had given birth to me, she had loved a man that had never experienced love and she was a bright and beautiful force of light to everyone she came in contact with. She may have never sold any of her art work or expressed herself in ways that I thought she could have, but she had definitely fulfilled upon a purpose greater than she could ever have imagined. I think sometimes us human beings get stuck in fantasies of grandeur, we believe that if we don't achieve something at the status of Martin Luther King, impact music like The Beatles or become the next Oprah that we have not succeeded in our lives purpose. We fantasize about speaking to the masses and spreading messages of love and being big, overly ambitious and overwhelmingly impressive, we don't take time to realize that our day to day encounters change the world. We don't realize that everything we do is a domino effect. That who we are and who we be from moment to moment and minute to minute determines so much about the people that inhabit our space. We don't really consider that we are all already great and all there is to do is be that expression of love and happiness She was evolved and wasn't really interested in dealing with the pettiness of the ego on this plane. She was ready to move to the next realm and that's just what she did.

They pulled the plug on her and the light shade of blue progressively got darker. A cold chill filled the air and I knew her spirit was gone. It was the first time I understood that the human body is nothing but a vessel, a container to hold our soul and spirit in. I always told my Mom that if anything ever happened to her I would kill myself. I was sixteen years old, my hormones were raging and something that I thought I would never in my wildest imagination be able to handle I handled. I do believe that its possible I was given this experience so early in my life to set me up powerfully for all that life would throw at me. Death has become something completely normal to me. Although there are only a select few I feel I could not handle the passing of, I really learned that everything in life is impermanent so you have to enjoy it all while its available to you. Learning this in the midst of teenage melancholy is truly a gift.

I am my Mother and I will be able to do all the things she never got to do. I have overcome most of the insecurities and negative self-talk that she had. I know that I am beautiful and am able to accept a compliment openly and honestly. I love myself. I am with a man who knows my worth. I will be financially free. I will not work at dead end jobs for the rest of my life. I will reach my highest potential and be able to express myself and be my full expression of creativity. I love my life and am committed to taking care of my body and health. I will not self-sabotage. I will not be brainwashed by society and it's impossible expectations. I will love myself and be in touch with the divine essence that I am. I learned everything I know from my Mother. Her SELF taught me how to be everything I could ever possibly dream of. I learned how to be everything I wanted to be but more importantly everything I didn't want to be. I love you Mom and want to thank you for giving me the opportunity and privilege that this life is.

CHAPTER 7

SOMETHING FOR NOTHING

I remember the first time the idea of stealing entered into my consciousness. I was a freshman in high school and a transient friend of mine told me she had been stealing chicken patty sandwiches from the lunch line. I should have known right then and there that she was no good, but instead I thought she was adventurous and rebellious. The concept of stealing was something that had never even crossed my mind up until that point but when she mentioned it something inside of me stirred and it felt like a new love was born. I entered the line with her and watched her work her magic. I was astounded, stunned, baffled and impressed when she actually got away with it. I thought, "How is this even possible!?"

This is how it all started, the beginning of my lies, deceit, and self-inflicted ridiculousness. It began with a sandwich and ended with stereo systems, kitchen tables, credit cards, and a year's supply of groceries. I stole paintings off of walls, and money out of wallets. Any employer that hired this suburban white girl got ripped off, scammed and stolen from by yours truly. Needless to say, it got pretty ugly.

Venture was my favorite store in the world when I was a child and teenager, especially the shoe department. My Grandma and I would always say Hello to Tony the cart guy at the entrance of the store. We would then proceed to eat some typical Venture type snacks in the stores café. You know the usual high fat, high carbohydrate, high fructose corn syrup food made with a bunch of unpronounceable ingredients. I always liked the pretzels with nacho cheese and we ate a lot of popcorn too. Come to think of it my Grandma actually worked in the jewelry department for a short stint.

The first thing I ever stole was a Jimi Hendrix CD and the only reason was because he wrote a song about the wind crying. At that age I thought Jimi was still alive and well. The way he played the guitar set my heart on fire. I was very disappointed when I came to find out that I was born in the wrong decade and Jimi had been gone for quite some time.

I walked into my favorite store, headed straight to the music section and prepared for the biggest thievery challenge I had had up until that point. I tore the metal tag off, shoved it in my purse and probably looked like the most suspicious person on the planet at that moment. I was sweating profusely and felt a rush of adrenaline surging through my veins. I looked left, right, up and down to assure that no one had just seen my move. I walked to the front door and marched right out of the store. I passed Tony and the metal detectors on the way out and neither one of them made a sound. As I saw the sunlight shining in the parking lot I turned around expecting that someone would be following me out to catch me. My pulse was fast and my forehead dripped with sweat, but as I turned around nobody was there. No one knew what had just happened. Just me, the CD and the universe. As I stood outside the store in awe I thought, "I can get things for NOTHING!?" A monster was born.

Years and years of stealing went on. It got to the point where I could steal just about anything from anywhere or anyone. Unfortunately, I was a natural born thief, better than a killer I thought. If I saw something that I wanted I would steal it. I'd go into the locker rooms in high school and go through people's purses and book bags and take their wallets. Sometimes if I liked their jacket or purse I'd just take the whole damn thing. One time I went into a store, put a kitchen table and stereo system in the cart and walked right out the door. I would go to the grocery store and get the most expensive meats, fish and produce and walk right out the door. An artist guy that I had a crush on that didn't even know I existed would put his paintings up around school, guess where they wound up: my apartment. I worked at a cd store and would have my friends come in and steal box set after box set of our favorite bands and music we didn't even know, but it was free so hey who cares!? I'd bring a book bag to a store fill it up with all the clothes I wanted and walk right out the door. I knew all the different types of metal detectors and devices that existed from working in retail myself.

At this time in my life I was a straight up obnoxious and defiant brat. I hated everything and had respect for nothing. I didn't think about there being any consequences associated with stealing. Of course somewhere in the back of my mind my Catholic school training had me thinking of the Ten Commandments and the, "thou shall not steal" rule but that was all made up anyway so it didn't really matter. It didn't even cross my mind that stealing stuff actually had an impact on people.

I remember one time when I had stolen from the locker room at school when a girl's gym class was going on. I had gone into a fellow classmate's unlocked locker and taken her whole wallet. Her ID's, credit cards, social security card and so on. Her friend's wallet was in the locker with hers and I decided to take that as well which also had all the aforementioned things in it. I was by myself when I executed this crime and walked outside immediately afterward to make sure everything was perfectly hidden in my backpack. When I walked back in, the class had been dismissed and I saw the two girls that I had just stolen from copiously crying to the high school gym teacher. As I passed by I heard them explaining to her that they had left the locker unlocked and now everything was gone. Both of them were so upset and sad.

It didn't faze me at all. I actually silently laughed to myself that I was the one that was responsible for that and had just caused all that drama. I guess I had not even a glimmer of the light in my being at that point. I just kept thinking how cool I was that I had just gotten away with something and would now be able to buy myself clothes and a concert ticket with money I didn't have to work for. I had no shame, no remorse and absolutely no respect.

I could go on and on about the tales of my stealing days but I think I have painted the picture quite clear. These are not things that I am happy or proud of but necessary to tell because of what I learned out of all of it and how it eventually made me wake up.

Looking back on things you did in the past can be a very hard thing to do. Most of us tend to grow up a bit, mature and even develop more consciousness and respect as we get older. I beat myself up for years for all the horrible things I did to people. It has become unfathomable to me that the girl that did that stuff was living in the body of the woman I am now.

Stealing is something I now cannot even understand and because of my experience of it, I know just how miserable it can and will make your life. I have had so many things stolen from me at different points. I can't even count on one hand how many times I've had to replace my license or my social security card. I can't recall how many times I've had to cancel debit cards. I've even had my identity stolen from me more than once. It is a true testament to what goes around comes around. The first couple things I got stolen from me I would get so pissed off about and somewhere along the line I realized that the universe was dishing up the same stuff that I had been throwing out. You reap what you sow was no longer just a stupid Bible quote.

CHAPTER 8

THE WAKE UP WATER

For some reason when I was a teenager I really wanted to live in Wrigleyville, the home of Wrigley field and some of the most annoyingly diehard baseball fans in the history of the game. It's more like a drunk frat party going on complete with slutty unknowing twenty something girls than anyone really having a love for the game. I didn't particularly like baseball but for some reason gravitated toward that part of the city. It was probably because it always seemed to be so busy and teeming with people my age. I wanted to be where the party was, even if it was people I would not consciously choose to party with.

My friend and I moved to a garden apartment (or basement apt as some would call it) in Wrigleyville and were paying about 750 dollars a month for rent, which was a steal for that neighborhood. I would quickly come to find out why it was so cheap. It was exciting to live in that part of town. Our apartment previous to that was in the city but felt more like it was on the outskirts. It was located in an area where not too many "cool" people lived and all our neighbors were older alcoholics and given up on life types. Our new abode was right in the middle of the hip part of town, had an el right by it, and better yet had some of the best bars and restaurants the city of Chicago had to offer, at least that's what my early twenties mentality thought.

Our apartment was very cute and quaint. It had a couple stairs going down to the front door and a long walkway to get to it. It was a very typical three level Chicago looking brick building. Our landlords were a married couple that lived upstairs with their kids who would stomp around at night. It had two bedrooms, a kitchen, bathroom and living room and was quite narrow with a low ceiling. It wasn't the most high class place but for the money you couldn't beat it. We had not yet grown out of posting band posters all over the wall as well as random pictures, quotes and sayings. I made curtains out of photographs and wrote sayings on the wall by connecting small pieces of masking tape together, My favorite was a song lyric from my favorite band that said, "Don't let the world bring you down, not everyone here is that fucked up and cooooold, remember why you came and while you're alive, experience the warmth before you go." That was my favorite lyric. I thought everyone was fucked up and cold and I was looking for my warmth.

Shoplifting was still running rampant in my life at this point in time and looking back I suspect I may have had a mild to slightly severe case of kleptomania. I would get an amazing rush from walking into stores and walking out with everything I wanted. When I lived in this apartment it got to be a little out of hand.

I remember this particular afternoon just like yesterday. I was sitting on the couch watching some three o'clock in the afternoon poor excuse for television type of program and marveling at how pretty much everything in my apartment with little exception was stolen. I was mentally patting myself on the back thinking about what a great thief I was. I looked at the multiple stereos I had-stolen. The kitchen table: stolen. The groceries in the fridge and freezer: stolen. All the beauty and hair supplies: stolen. The clothes in my closet: stolen. DVDs and CDs: stolen. I mean about 90% of the things in this apartment never made it to the check-out line at a number of given stores. They were secretly removed from local and non- local grocery stores, corporations and businesses by me. I sat back and marveled at my accomplishments. For a girl who didn't make that much money I certainly had some nice things.

I continued watching the idiot box with the idiot show on and saw an emergency broadcast message flash upon the screen. Apparently a severe storm system was about to move through the Chicago metropolitan area and was going to deliver very high winds, torrential downpours, fatal lightning and possible tornadoes. As the screen flashed its urgent message I looked out the window and observed the clouds getting darker and darker, the clouds seemed to be literally rolling in and were a black greenish color. The rain started.

Ever since I was a child I was both terrified and fascinated by storms. At one point I even wanted to be a meteorologist and a storm chaser. I wanted to be on the channel 7 news at 10 and take over for my local weatherman. I imagined myself old and sophisticated informing everyone of what type of clothing they would have to be wearing that day. When I discovered that they weren't actually standing in front of a map of the United States and instead in front of a green screen that dream died. I mean it seemed very complicated and I was certain you had to have a high proficiency of calculus to figure out mathematical equations for the distances of upcoming storms. You needed to learn the difference between nimbus, cumulonimbus and stratus and had to know what a jet stream was and why tornadoes were caused and how hurricanes get their names and it all just seemed too overwhelming, besides I was never any good with numbers and didn't really think I was cute enough to be on TV. Another abandoned dream.

As I'm staring out the window of my garden apartment the sky got thick and black and the rain stared pouring in a manner I had never encountered until then. It was SO loud! It sounded like pinballs were falling from the sky at five hundred miles an hour. It was torrential and just came down in buckets and buckets. It was absolutely unbelievable. It just kept going and going. Usually with a storm like that it'll pour for a minute or two and then ease up, but no, this was some type of hyperactivity storm cell that needed to cry a river if not an ocean.

I sat on the couch with my feet up watching this remarkable display that Mother Nature was putting on for me. Lightning, thunder the whole works. I got up to go to the bathroom and stepped into a puddle, I was quite confused. As I stood up I looked down and saw the bottom of the couch was getting drenched and my feet were now ankle deep in water. I looked over to the wall in front of me and the water started gushing like a volcano that had been dormant for a hundred years. I was paralyzed. My first thought was, "wow, this water feels so nice and cold". It had been 90 degrees that day and it was quite refreshing seeing that I lived in un air conditioned premises. I started laughing. Laughing to me is what crying is to other people. In panic moments

I am more likely to laugh then cry. I have come to find it's basically the same emotion anyway.

I stood in the middle of my apartment paralyzed with fear, laughing, not able to move and not knowing what the hell to do. I really wished my roommate was home. I quickly tried to unplug everything I could as I didn't really want my final day on planet earth to be proceeded by an electrocution. By this time the water had gotten to about my mid shin and I headed toward my front door slowly but surely. Clothes and CDS that were on the floor were floating and a box filled with all my grade school photos and bozo the clown picture were dying a slow death: Drowning clowns and underwear. I made it to the door and noticed even more water coming in there. I slowly turned the knob and cracked it up a tiny bit when a giant surge of water whacked the door completely open and threw me backwards. I was definitely not expecting that. It had really gotten ridiculous at this point.

I ran upstairs sprinting speed to my landlord's house. I was impressed with how fast I could move in emergency situations. I pounded on the door in somewhat of a maniacal style and no one answered. I ran to my upstairs neighbors who were two guitar playing potheads so I really didn't expect much out of them. As suspected, no answer. Probably too busy listening to classic rock and smoking joints.

By this time that rain had calmed significantly and the clouds were passing fast. The sun was breaking its way through the clouds to reveal a prismatic display of ROYGBIV. I was experiencing all this by myself and was so upset that even after me telling the story no one could ever really get the full scope of what I had just encountered, no one would ever understand the emotional rollercoaster I just rode. Still laughing at this point because now I had actually really considered it funny, I waded in water past my knees down the pathway to my front door. The door had somehow shut and I had to push it open. Water is beyond heavy and I really had wished I had an innertube or raft. I splashed through the water and the first thing I saw when I got into the house was my mattress floating. Papers, pictures, CDs, DVDs and anything that was even remotely near to the floor had gone under. Many if not most or all of my stolen items had sunk to their bloody or shall I say watery death.

I sat outside on the front steps of the apartment building waiting for someone to get home whether it be my roommate who I had tried to call to no avail, my guitar playing pothead neighbors or the noisy children landlords. No one came for quite awhile. While I waited I contemplated on the happenings that had just transpired. It became quite clear to me what had happened or rather my perception of what had just happened.

Life always knows what is going on with you and it will give you those experiences that will either grow you, evolve you or awake you, however it all depends on whether you choose to listen or not. I was sleeping at this point in my life, completely oblivious to the implications of stealing, completely oblivious to karma and all its repercussions. I had not known that my actions actually had consequences. I had not known that taking things that did not belong to me messed with the flow of everything. Right before this flood happened I had been sitting around idolizing myself for my thievery. It is a law of nature that you will always get what you deserve and that whatever you do will come right back to you and maybe even ten-fold sometimes. It took a foot of cold water, an awful musty smell, swarm of mosquitoes and destruction of my personal property for me to get this concept. I never stole a day after that and learned the most cliché of all sayings "you get what you give." I was giving dishonesty, disrespect and dishonor to life so it gave me back destruction and damage. It destroyed that which was incorrect in my actions. I am truly blessed to have learned at a very young age that you ALWAYS get what you deserve, and once you wake up you can use this law to have everything and more than you think is possible for yourself.

CHAPTER 9

LOSING IRENE

Irene had been my best friend since fourth grade. We did lots of typical girl things together like going to the mall and eating ice cream. We would make up songs, sing along to broad way soundtracks and have crushes on the same types of boys. Naturally when we were about 21 it was a great idea for us to go to South America together when she suggested it. She had been there already. She wanted to go back to improve her Spanish and get some more life experience under her belt. Plus the idea of meeting a Latin man and falling madly in love and having romantic affairs was clearly something we would have both been majorly interested in.

When we were in high school, Irene revealed to me one day in a very teary display that her Father who was a prominent lawyer was a cocaine addict. My first thought was, "That makes a lot of sense because he is always making weird snorting and hacking sounds," my second reaction was, "Wow, I can't believe it." Up until that point I had thought of her family as very nuclear and perfect seeming. Her brother, sister and her were all straight A honor roll students, they were all super athletic and never got into any trouble in school. Her Mom was a substitute teacher and they just all seemed so impeccable and smart to me. This was truly a wake-up call to looks being more than deceiving. From that point on I felt I had awoken to see things and people as they really are. I found that all these families and people I deemed as perfect all had their own battles, struggles, dramas, and hardships. It's as if I thought I was the only one who had problems up until that point.

After years of friendship and dealing with things together we set off to South America, actually we went to Mexico first and that was where the problems began. This was at a very immature and childish time and I had thought that something was wrong with Irene. I thought she had a long stick up her ass which she was unwilling to remove and just have a little fun. I was going to make sure that we not only had fun but a lot of it, early twenties reckless abandon fun.

In Mexico, Acapulco to be exact we went to take a TEFL course so that we could get certified to teach English in a different country. I was just excited to be in Mexico and to drink and party, she was mostly business with a splash of fun from my perspective, which looking back makes a whole world of sense, I mean after all we had gone there with an intention in mind. We stayed at a teacher's house that she had hooked us up with from doing research online and he was a really great guy. He was also all business with a splash or I'd be willing to say a droplet of fun.

We went to the school that the teacher worked at and he let us sit in and watch him do his thing. He would lead us through English courses at his house. I believe we were there for about two weeks learning past participles and conjugations and so on.

Within the couple of weeks that we were there I made sure that we had some of those reckless abandon times I spoke of earlier, we found bars that shot tequila straight in to your mouth and went to a very high class club that was just across the street from where we were staying. I can't even remember how many men I made out with on that trip. Needless to say, I wasn't too classy.

We went to a bar on the beach one night and after having a couple rounds and a few shots of tequila we started talking to a group of guys that were Mexican but looked more American than anything else. They seemed to be quite respectable and one of them told me that his Dad was an architect and owned a mansion on the water. I didn't believe him until we got there.

I didn't really grasp where we were until the next morning when I woke up in a huge bed in a huge room and saw the ocean out the window. I felt confident about who I was with seeing that he had completely respected my rejection to his sexual advances the previous night. Also, he was in a separate bed that was next to mine and all my clothes were intact. Good sign. I awoke and went downstairs, but not before going down a winding staircase around the outside of the house, I felt like a princess in a castle. When I arrived to the breakfast table, there was a maid serving eggs, bacon, oatmeal, pancakes, toast and pretty much every breakfast food available to planet earth with a variety of fresh squeezed juices. I felt like a celebrity, I didn't realize that things like this actually existed. I mean I grew up in a Roseanne type house in the less well off part of a middle class suburban town where my family worked hard for their money and probably didn't even imagine things like this. I sat down at the breakfast table and looked out upon the Pacific Ocean and all its majesty. His Father, the architect had built a lavish and Salvador Dali-esque looking pool that bled right into the Ocean. I kept on trying to wake myself up and kept realizing I was already awake. Incredible. Irene joined us for our excessive and elaborate breakfast with the guy she had spent the night with in a different wing of the mansion. I had broken my camera a few days before and was beyond pissed that I was getting no photo documentation of this extravagant event.

We spent the rest of the morning with the boys and made plans for the following evening. One of the guys drove us home in his very expensive foreign convertible. I kept wondering why I was getting to experience this. I mean I certainly was no model material and neither was Irene. We were just good wholesome American girls.

We met the guys the next night at a club down the road from where we were staying and I proceeded to get excessively drunk upon arriving. After a couple hours of dancing and having fake conversations with who knows who, I decided to go back to the dream mansion with one of the guys and left Irene behind at the club. In my drunken state I did not call her and let her know where I was. I woke up in the morning, this time in bed with the guy however clothes still intact (thank God) and re did the same thing I had done the day before with the breakfast and the maid and the view and the castle, only Irene was not there this time. For one reason or another, the thought that she would be worried about me never even entered my mind. It didn't even occur to me that I should call her and let her know that I'd be home in awhile. I decided to eat my royal breakfast, go for a swim in the ornate pool and hang out with my new found handsome and wealthy male friends. Many hours of lollygagging around and I had the expensive car guy drive me home, even though I didn't know where home was. I knew it was by the Wal-Mart and that's about it so I had him take me there.

We cruised at fast speeds down the calles and I sensed us getting closer to home, I saw Irene walking towards the Wal-Mart we had just passed and she looked severely distressed and frantic. I had him stop the car immediately, said my goodbye and proceeded to run back after her calling her name out loud. When she turned around I was not expecting the response I got which was somewhere in between a screaming-crying-pissed off with a hue of relief and happiness fit. She started yelling at me about how irresponsible I was and that she was scared and was left all by herself. I'm not sure why I didn't realize it wasn't cool to leave your best friend by herself, especially in a foreign country. Needless to say our friendship was never the same after that and I'm pretty sure she gotten taken advantage or even violated that night although it was never discussed. What was worse was my lack of empathy and compassion. I tried to turn the tables and make it like it was her fault for not being more independent and self-sufficient. I made it seem like she was ruining my time and spoiling all my fun. At that time I thought I was right and she was wrong. I felt annoyed that she didn't want to act like a child and be crazy with me. I felt frustrated that at the age of 21 she was so adult like and had her shit together because I sure as hell didn't. This was the beginning of the demise of our friendship and the end of a many year connection. This was the time that I trained my best friend not to trust or respect me. Many other incidences occurred when we ventured to South America. The immaturity, stupidity and irresponsibility continued and got even worse. I eventually became so disrespectful and childish that I just completely cut off the friendship and never spoke to her again. We were 2000 miles away from home and I just decided to leave her behind and stay with new friends that I had made. I didn't see it then but now it is obvious just how insanely huge my ego was at that time. I didn't know how to have conflict resolution conversations or how to say how I really felt. I knew how to be scared and jealous of my friend. I knew that what I wanted more than anything underneath all my childishness was to be mature and smart like her. I wanted the confidence, the athleticism, the beauty, the body and the brains and I didn't believe that I had any of it. My own lack of self-love caused me to push an amazing woman and friend away. She had invited me there to grow and learn and expand myself and I took that opportunity and tossed it in the trash. Ten years later I can see it all for what it really is which was a profound learning experience and the foundation for me becoming and working hard at the woman I am today. I still miss her sometimes and plan on someday reuniting.

CHAPTER 10

WHEREVER YOU GO....

When I was 22 I moved to South America, Chile to be exact, Santiago to be exacter. My friend, Irene from grade school had studied abroad and already made the trek there and had wanted to visit again and chose to invite me along. Although at this age it was the adventure of a lifetime, I soon found out that what people say is true. The grass wasn't any greener there and even though I had a different environment, I was still me. What I'd really done was try to run away from my life, my insecurities and my problems.

At this point in my life I hated people, I hated my job, I hated my life and more than anything I hated myself. The idea of moving somewhere foreign was so idealistic and romantic. I would find my Latin lover, my perfect job, learn espanol, and have an exciting well-traveled eccentric circle of friends. I would be happy.

I had been looking to get away from all the people I was always comparing myself to. The skinny bitches, the beautiful woman, the people who were all better and smarter than me, which I thought was pretty much everybody. I wanted to leave them all behind and go find people who were on my level (which is interesting because even though I thought everyone was superior to me, I also thought they were inferior.) I wanted to find people on my wavelength of thinking. I wanted to desert the busboy from my work that fed me cocaine and crystal meth. I really wanted to take a hike from my anger and failure. I didn't want to deal with the fact that I had lost my Mother six years earlier. I just wanted to get away from the country I disliked so much, the country that was filled with greed, superficial thinking and unconsciousness. I didn't realize at the time that I was the unconsciousness and the source of my own misery. How in the world would a 22 year know such a thing?

I wanted to get away from My Grandma and Uncle who from my point of view appeared to have given up on their lives. My Grandma would spend her days watching soap operas, ordering unnecessary things from the home shopping network and watching fear based news broadcasts. She never really left the house much once I was a teenager. Looking back, I'm pretty sure she had some type of anxiety or panic disorder. The older she got, the more scared she got. Her life was over after my Grandfather died and that energy leaked on to me. It was her fault and I needed to get away from her.

My Uncle is and was quite the character. He spent most of his time hiding out from his homosexuality. He worked two or three jobs at a time and created a life where he was constantly distracted and didn't have to deal with himself. I remember always feeling so awful for him. He would work his ass off and never really have that much money. My Grandma would buy things she didn't have money for and he would end up paying for them. It was as if he had replaced my Grandfather. I always knew he was gay, at least from the time I even knew what that was. My Mother knew too, we would talk about it and even asked him a few times. He would just get outraged and say that he couldn't believe that we would ask him such a thing. He would get majorly offended. My Grandma played dumb and acted like she didn't know and because of this I suspect he did not ever come out to her until a couple years before she passed on. Anyways:

The same cast of characters showed up in South America, the same type of scenery, the same conversations, jealousies, gossip, dramatics and miseries. It didn't take me too long to see that people are the same everywhere. There will always be gossip, there will always be fakeness and most of all there will always be people preaching about how their point of view is the right point of view. Minus traditions and culture...humans are humans. I met activists, idiots, America obsessed people and haters. Sometimes I would pretend I was Canadian just so I didn't have to explain myself. I taught English at an Institute where all age groups and walks of life attended. They really didn't train their teachers well and to this day I am not exactly sure how the hell I got hired. They must have been desperate. I had little to no Spanish speaking skills and zero experience in that type of work environment. For some reason they didn't want people who spoke Spanish, they wanted strictly English native speakers. My thinking was if you can't speak Spanish how the hell are you supposed to translate English? I just decided to go with it. The only thing I knew how to do was wait on tables and fake a smile. I'm sure the fake smiling came in handy when they were interviewing me. It took them a couple days to decide if I would get the position. I was more than elated when I got hired considering that I was about broke and literally picking oranges off of trees to eat.

My first day of training was terrifying, and my first day of being in front of a classroom even more. I had no clue what I was doing but was somewhat relieved when they told me they were placing me in the higher level English classes. These were the classes where the students already had some previous competency and knowledge of and in the English language.

Yes, I speak English, but why? I don't know. I suppose it because that's what I grew up with. I was always good in writing classes in school but when it came to breaking down why and how the words and phrases I was speaking were coming out of my mouth I had not the slightest clue. Past participle and conjugations became my mortal enemy. I was supposed to be teaching something I didn't even understand. Luckily, I was a master of bullshitting. My favorite classes to teach were the "free" classes which were basically just that, free to talk about anything conversational. Free topic and free speaking. We were directed to never ever speak of things such as religion, politics, or sex. I'm pretty sure at some point I ended up talking about all these things with my students. I asked my students one day what their view of The United States and Americans were. They were more than happy to respond.

It was quite entertaining to hear the different interpretations that people had of the US and Americans, I mean the ones who had never visited and even the ones that did. It seems a lot of them thought that Americans lived in some type of permanent 90210- lifestyle. They suspected that Hollywood spanned the entire 50 states and that every woman was a bombshell and had breast implants and that every guy was some hot beer guzzling fratty looking type. Oh yes, life in the United States was an undying and never ending hedonistic party! Apparently these people had been exposed to one too many teeny bopper type movies.

The other category of people hated Americans to their core and for good reason. We were the reason for so many of their political and social issues. Americans were greedy, materialistic and uneducated buffoons. Americans and their gluttony were the problem with the world. We didn't care about anyone but ourselves and our President looked like a monkey. It's obvious what people I connected more with.

This may be obvious to some of you, but most of us fantasize, romanticize, or even believe that if we move to a different city, state, or even country things will be better and people will even be nicer. Opportunities will be more readily available if we could just get the hell away from the people we don't like. Well guess what? Those people will show up again and again just with different faces and until you learn what you're supposed to learn from them they'll stick around. They may have different names and faces and sometimes even gender, however the same personality types that cause you trouble will show up again and again until you learn how to effectively deal with them.

My short year that I spent in South America was filled with amazing scenery, brilliant people and the same habits, and issues I had back home. I tried to run away from a drug habit I acquired only to find myself that much closer to Colombia. I lost my best friend that I went down there with due to my lack of respect for her. I ended up having to come back because I had made myself physically ill. I found a guy I was in love with and I was pretty sure loved me equally and I proceeded to push him away. Every way of thinking and being that I was back home showed up again and again and again and sometimes now that I look back I believe it was even more amplified. What I had been trying to run away from I ran right into and I thank life for giving me that experience. I learned so much about myself and what is important to me. We have all heard the quote "Wherever you go, there you are." I had to travel two thousand miles to figure that out for myself.

CHAPTER 11

TERATOMA

I looked like I was nine months pregnant. That would be impossible though. I hadn't slept with anyone and had never even had a boyfriend. My stomach had become so distended I couldn't even see my feet anymore. All of this had happened in the course of a month. I had been partying and doing drugs more than normal so I figured it was just a beer belly. I thought maybe I was getting fat because of all the late night drunken burritos and pizza I was eating. It seemed to have sprung up overnight though. When I would take public transportation men would get out of their seats to let me sit down because they thought I was pregnant. I just went into denial about it for a month or so

I started getting feverish and just feeling weird. It was indescribable. I just didn't feel right. Nothing in particular felt off besides everything.

I was still in Chile and living with a fellow co-worker and friend, Carol in her apartment. People had definitely started to take notice of my stomach. I was so angry because I had just lost a bunch of weight and here I was getting fat again. My friend finally said I better go to the doctor which was kind of unrealistic considering I was so broke. I would pick fruit off of trees because I didn't have money to buy food, so a doctor kind of seemed out of the question. Carol agreed to pay for it because she was pretty well off and had family there.

I went to the doctor and they told me I was pregnant. I didn't quite know what to think. I mean I was a virgin, I had never had sex and I was pregnant? Must be another case of immaculate conception. Obviously, that couldn't be the case so we went to another doctor who came to the same conclusion. I told them that was impossible and they admitted they had no idea. They had never seen anything like it before.

I opted to go home to deal with this pesky problem in my country of origin. My Grandma and Uncle who I hadn't seen in a year picked me up at the airport. It was bittersweet. I was pissed off to be back home and at the same time had a sense of overwhelming relief seeing them both. The next day we headed to the doctor who still had no clue what was going on. A few doctor's visits and hundreds of dollars later they concluded that I had a teratoma.

Teratoma literally means "monster tumor" in Greek. One doctor even told me that it's pretty much my body trying to create a baby by itself. In my 23 year old mind it didn't seem like it was that big of a deal. I thought just cut the damn thing out and lets be done with it. I had no idea that it could have been cancerous or that any complications could have arisen. Thank God for a young mind dealing with that. If that was now I'd probably be thinking I was going to die.

Doctors and researchers have no evidence of just how or why people get these monster tumors. There is really no known real reason. They know that it is a germ cell tumor which I guess would mean you have a very germy body?

The night before my surgery, I had to drink some disgusting concoction of liquid stuff to clean out my digestive system. I cannot recall anything I have ever tasted worse than that. I came to find I was supposed to dilute it with water. Oops.

The morning of my surgery I don't really remember being that afraid at all. They took me in, got me prepped and it was done. The next thing I remember is waking up and looking at the clock on the wall. It seemed to be all types of distorted, I knew it was a clock but didn't look like it. The hands were backwards and the numbers were not in order. Anesthesia is such an intriguing thing. A nurse popped in to check on me and I started yelling at her that she had stolen my uterus and I wanted it back. I clearly was out of it.

When I finally came out of my drug induced stupor, they put me in a hospital room where my Grandma and Uncle came to visit me. When my Uncle came in the first thing he told me was that the tumor was 25 pounds. I knew my Uncle was an exaggerative being so when the doctor came in I asked him. Turns out he wasn't embellishing the truth this time around.

I had had a twenty-five pound monster tumor attached to my right ovary. How this happened I do not know but I have some interesting theories about it.

At that point in my life, up to and leading to before I had gotten diagnosed with the Teratoma, I was living like there was no tomorrow. I had developed a few pesky drug habits and drank whenever I wanted to. I didn't just drink to have a drink, I drank like a teenager and early twenty- something would. I drank to get drunk and not just buzzed, but black out drunk. I had no concept of what nutrition was. I thought iceberg lettuce was nutritious and meant I was being healthy. My daily intake of food consisted mostly of those fast food names we all know well. Not just once a day, but multiple times a day. I clearly did not have a high opinion of myself when I was younger. The things I really wanted I did not tell people about. I was living like an island being completely untrue to myself and the people around me. I deprived myself of love and true friendship. I told myself that I was worthless and would never be able to have the things I want. I thought I was so different from everyone else on the planet. I was suffering and everyone else was happy. All of that can tell you just a little bit about how selfish I was. I abused and even tortured my body by depriving it of true nourishment, not only physically but mentally, emotionally, and spiritually, ultimately holistically. I mistreated and neglected my body, mind and soul. The things I put in my body were a direct reflection of the amount of love I had for myself

The body is an insanely intelligent machine and will tell you and give you warning when you are not giving it the respect it deserves. It truly is a temple and when that temple is not being honored it will not honor you. I am very fortunate to have learned this lesson at such a young age. I learned that what you are putting in will show up on the outside. I learned that optimal health and well- being is directly parallel to the amount of self-love you have. I am fortunate.

CHAPTER 12

JEW FOR A FEW

I never knew my father. Never even knew his name until I was about ten or eleven. When I finally found out his name, the detective in me was born. My Mother told me his name was Martin, he was Jewish and lived in a suburb close to ours.

It didn't really bother me much until I was in about fourth grade. I had come to find that most people in my school had Fathers and I wondered why I was different? I approached my Mother about it and she had told me a dramatic encounter of their seemingly soulmatic relationship. He was apparently very romantic and handsome; also a musician. That is a lethal combination for us women. My Grandma told me how he would bring over champagne and chocolate for my Mom. They had spent many passionate evenings together until my Mom had found out that she was pregnant. Apparently his family was very affluent and told him they would cut him off from the family and their money if he decided to marry my Mother. He was only 19 at the time and a total pothead.

The events that ensued were my Mother birthing me and him signing some document about how he had no legal rights to me whatsoever. She never saw him again after that. I was raised fatherless which definitely helped contribute to my eventual hatred of men, which took a whole lifetime to alter. I wondered though who this mystery man was and just where I came from? Who was this other half of human being that I didn't know existed? I decided to go on a quest.

In grade school we used to sell candy bars to make money for our Catholic school. I was always great at it. I would stand in front of the local convenience store and sell my little butt off. I remember most of the time it was icy cold outside which I think made people take pity on me. I always wore the same plastic purple clip in my hair, convinced it would bring me luck. We won prizes for whoever sold the most candy, however I can't remember exactly what we won. An idea occurred to me one night while standing in front of the fluorescent lit pantry. I could find my Dads address and go sell candy at his front door. He would have no clue who I was. I could just see what he looks like and be done with it.

The next weekend my best friend Irene and I got on our bicycles, candy bars in tow and biked an hour away to his house address or at least what I thought was his address that I found in the yellow pages. This was before technology was all pervasive. We arrived on his block and mustered up the courage to finally go and ring the doorbell. No one answered. I checked in the windows and snooped all around the house to find that no one was home. "What a wasted trip," I thought. For one reason or another we never went back and I decided to just give up on my dreams of meeting my Father. Until:

High school came around and I met my new best friend Tanya...certainly by now many many suns had passed but I still had a deep seeded "I need to know my father" issue going on. By now technology had picked up quite a bit so we were able to do a people search on the Internet. We found out where he went to high school and promptly went there to look at year books from the year he had graduated. Of course he decided to not take his picture that year. Tanya and I found out where he worked because they had a directory of what alumni were doing now. We drove to the place he supposedly worked and it was no longer in existence. Once again, I had hit a dead end and decided to give it up. Until:

I got drunk. Real drunk. Sixteen year old drunk. I was hanging out a friend's house in the city and we were drunk and stoned talking about life stuff. Somehow my Dad came up and I told everyone the story about him that my Mom had told me. I had been carrying around the one lone blurry foggy picture my Mom had of him, her and his band members for years in my wallet. I had also managed to acquire a phone number somehow. I decided it would be a really great idea to call his house. So I did.

There is nothing like a little bit of liquid courage to make you lose all your maturity and responsibility. The phone rang and rang and on about the fifth ring an elderly fellow answered the phone. I said, "Hello, may I please speak with Martin Steinburg?" trying to sound as mature and sober as possible. He said, "Martin doesn't live here anymore, but may I ask who is calling?" I said loud and kind of belligerently "YES! This is his daughter!!!"...a long and I mean loooong pause followed. And then a dial tone.

Being as drunk as I was that was not going to be the end of it. I picked up, dialed again and after about two rings the same man answered. He didn't even say hello and instead screamed, "I don't know what you want with Martin, he wants nothing to do with you, don't ever call back here again, don't ever EVER call back here again!" I figured out that the man with whom I was speaking must have been my Grandfather. He seemed really scared of me. I managed to fight back tears and anger and without even thinking yelled, "FUCK YOU asshole! You're a fucking asshole." Needless to say, it was a very immature interaction. I then hung up and put my father on the backburner of my mind. Until:

I was 25 years old and in a personal development course that my friend had been raving about for a year. It was three and a half days and supposedly assisted in working out all your unresolved issues. On the second day of this course I realized that I had major abandonment issues. I mean I had already known that just not the depth. At this point in my life I was 25 years old and had never been in a serious relationship let alone even had a boyfriend. I was terrified of men and had no clue about how to interact with them nor did I really want to. I believed that they were all pigs and all they were interested in was sex. I believed that I was unwanted and that's why my Father was never in the picture. If my Father didn't want me why would any other man on the planet want me? Obviously, a lot of stuff came up for me that weekend. I decided now with the major advancements in technology that it would be super simple to find him. I wanted to conquer these issues and in my mind meeting him was the only way that could ever happen. I went home on the Saturday night of the course, found his address on the internet and composed a letter. The following Monday it took me about four hours to mail it. I kept on walking to the mailbox and then turning around. I knew this was it. I knew that this was his real address and that this letter was being sent directly to him with my phone number on it. Martin Steinburg and I would finally have made contact. I was petrified and beyond excited. I mailed the letter.

A week later I was headed into a concert with some friends from work. As we were walking into the venue I got a call from an unknown number which didn't really phase me considering I was up to my neck in credit card debt. I headed to the bathroom and punched in my code to listen to my voicemails and I heard his voice for the first time. "Hi, uh uh, this is Martin, your Father uh uh I received your letter in the mail and uh uh would really like to talk uh uh, give me a call when you have a free uh uh moment." And he left me his number. I really wish someone would have been tape recording my face at that moment. It was fear, ecstasy, excitement, anger and madness all rolled up into one emotion. I had never been so ecstatic in all my life. He actually called me. He actually did exist! The other half of who created my existence on this here planet had finally made contact.

Our first conversation on the phone was inarguably the most awkward conversation I have ever had or ever will have. I can't recall it exactly, but I know we spoke mostly of superficial things like what we do for a living, what kind of hobbies we have and if I believe in Jesus. Yes, this devout Jewish man that my Mother had told me about was actually a born again Christian. I have no problem with people believing what they want to believe but please do not impose your views on me. You can tell me your views but don't act like they are the truth for me as well. A lot of our conversation revolved around him asking God for help around this situation and reading Bible quotes and such. It was all fine with me. I was talking to my Dad.

He had been married for many years now and had two boys that were now 16 and 18. He lived in a burb that was literally about 20 minutes away from where I currently resided. After a few awkward and forced phone calls we decided we were going to meet. He wanted me to meet him on Sunday morning at a Bible chapel he went to. Against all I believe in I decided to go and meet him. I may not be Christian or read the Bible but I am certainly open to other people's points of view even though some seem ridiculous to me. So Sunday was on and he was going to bring his wife.

I arrived to the chapel about 45 minutes early. I wanted to scope things out and observe all the brainwashed weirdo people that were there. This was no chapel or altar. It was some type of mega church. I saw the bands preparing for the stage and the singers warming up. This place must have fit a couple thousand people and was definitely not what I was expecting. I went and looked around the book shop and kept looking at the time. Eventually it was time to go find him waiting outside the church doors in the lobby. I had no clue what he looked like, so I just looked for people who were looking for people. I spotted them before they spotted me and composed myself. My heart was racing and I thought it was really unfair that he had someone there for support and I didn't. I approached them.

"H-Hi, Martin?" I said shyly and unsure. He said, "Hi, this is my wife Diane." We gave each other the guinness book of world records most strange and awkward hug. It felt so strange that all these years of wondering and investigating had let up to this one moment. It reminded me of Olympic athletes who spend their whole life training and practicing for that one minute race. This man that stood in front of me had no idea all the years I had wondered, fantasized, dreamed and thought of him and here he was in the flesh. I almost started to cry but held back my sentiments.

We proceeded into the church and I endured an hour of Bible passages, people being dunked in holy water and puberty stricken teenagers singing with their guitars. Obviously due to where we were we didn't talk much. It was like going to a movie on a first date. Pretty stupid.

When the mass ended we chit chatted once more and decided to go get some breakfast where we chit chatted some more. We found out some things we had in common and I learned about his life and him about mine. I think I may have occurred as somewhat of a wild child considering the jobs I had had and that I moved out of the country for a year. I mean these were dull suburban lifestyle people I was dealing with here so it seemed. We decided to meet again in the near future and we did.

I started to actually have a relationship with my Father at the age of 25 years old. It was very peculiar but also very rewarding. I still can't believe that I was brave enough to contact and go and meet him by myself I had so many judgments and so much weirdness about him it still baffles me that it was so desperately important for me to meet him. We started talking to each other on the phone a couple times a month and his wife and he actually gave me a birthday and Christmas present one year. I met and hung out with his two kids on a couple occasions. They helped my roommate and I move into our new apartment and really were good people to me. Naturally all the questions I had wanted answers to for years came up like, "Were you in love with my Mom?","How long were you together?", "Did you ever want to meet me?", "Did you ever think about me?", "Why didn't you ever contact me?" and a plethora of others. I got all my answers. For two or three years we had solid communication going on. I really didn't know where to take it from there. I mean I didn't really expect to even get as far as we did. I didn't even know if I wanted a relationship with this somewhat stranger of a man. As a result of both of us not really knowing where to take this new relationship, we fell out of communication for about a year. Once again I felt bothered.

I wrote another letter. I needed closure. I have never been good at cutting it off with people. I have done it quite a bit in my lifetime, however this was a different case. I had worked long and hard on this man and I wasn't willing to just let it dissipate in the wind. I either needed something created between us or a goodbye nice meeting ya. So I wrote him yet another letter.

Dear Martin,

Hi, How have you been? It's been quite a long time since we corresponded. I was just wondering what's been going on with you? We kind of left things hanging a little bit and I'm not quite sure where you are or how you feel about everything? I think we should either create something for our relationship or at the very least get some type of closure. Let me know how you feel about all this?

Love,
Natalie

About two weeks later I got a written response back in the mail.....

Dear Natalie,

How have you been? Thank you for writing the letter you did. I have been thinking about the same things you have. I don't know exactly what the objective of meeting me was or exactly what you wanted to get out of meeting me? There is something I should have told you from the beginning but was scared to bring up. I have had questions regarding my paternity. There were a few weeks that were a bit off by my calculation when I was dating your Mother. I was away at school for a few weeks in the time that she had gotten pregnant and always wondered if she had been with someone else? I would love to get a DNA test so that we can finally put this to rest and we can find out the truth. I am sure I am mistaken, but I'd like to us to know so we can make it legal. Please let me know if you would be willing to do this?

Martin

We met again, just him and I this time. This was the first time we were by ourselves. He had brought his security blanket all the previous times. We went to a DNA test place and they swabbed the inside of our mouths with cotton swabs. They had to send them out and gave us a code to call them back in a week to find out the results. We left and went out to breakfast and then I hopped on a train back to the city.

A week passed and I had not heard from him. I had pretty much put the test out of my mind because I knew the results. I mean it was obvious we even looked alike. I ended up calling the lab a couple days later just to hear the obvious results. I gave the woman my code and she told me "Martin Steinburg is excluded as the Father of the client specified according to our findings." I asked her to repeat and she did. I said goodbye and hung up the phone. Stunned, baffled, puzzled...HUH???

I called Martin kind of angry because I assumed that he had already called and found out. When he answered he said he had not called. I told him to call and then call me back. He did just that and was just as if not more confused than me. In that moment I felt worse for him than I did for myself. He had spent 29 years thinking he had a daughter, 25 of those years feeling guilt and shame over it to come to find that I wasn't even really his? I immediately got pissed at my long gone Mother and started making up all types on conspiracy theories. Did she know he wasn't the Father? Did she lie to him? Did she have a one night stand and not want to admit it? Was she cheating on him? Was she raped? Did she know who the real Father was but wanted him to be the Father so she could trap him? I felt 8000 miles away from the truth and still do. I will never know who my real Father is because chances are he doesn't even know I exist.

Our last conversation we had was when we discovered the results of the test. I had been hanging out with my Moms ex-boyfriend for the past four years, now viewed my Mother as a possible liar and/or whore and was no closer to meeting the other half of my creation. My parting words with Martin were this, "Thank you for being like a Father to me for these past few years, even though you weren't the real deal, just me thinking you were really had me grow. As a result of you I am now over my fear of men and relationships and since meeting you I am now in my first serious relationship. Even though you're not my real Father you helped me immensely. Thank you, I can now move on." There is no way for me to know who my real Father is unless some miracle happens and although some days I still get upset by it, I have come to accept it. Sometimes being in the unknowingness of life can serve a huge purpose. Mission accomplished.

CHAPTER 13

I'LL START NEXT MONDAY

I never had any clue about food, what was good for me and what was not. I grew up on fast food, donuts and homemade popcorn with a pound of butter on it (literally.) We were products of the 80 s. Instant gratification microwaving never sitting down at the dinner table type folks. Anything that was instant we ate.

Everyone in my family was overweight at some point. It seemed that we all teeter tottered. My Grandma eventually got to be so big that one of my fellow schoolmates once asked me if she was pregnant. I really paid no attention at all until about fourth grade when I acquired a bruise on my tummy from playing on the playground at school. When I lifted my shirt up and showed my Uncle he said, "Oh you're getting a nice roll there, better watch out." My lifelong obsession with the scale began.

I always remember being bigger than everyone. All the girls in grade school seemed to be so tiny and fragile while I was kind of hearty and meaty. My school uniform definitely didn't look the same on me as it did on them and most times I would wear sweatpants under my skirt just to hide my fat legs... even in the summer. My self-consciousness inhibited me from many activities. If anyone ever asked me to go swimming or to the beach I would make up an excuse and say I'm sick or I wasn't allowed to. No way was I going to let anyone see my fat body.

It only got worse as I went to high school. The way I wanted to dress was not available to me because cute clothes were only made for size 5's back then. I turned into somewhat of a tomboy for a short time even though it was never truly me, I would come to find years later that I'm more girly than I ever suspected.

I was happy when I started listening to punk, rock and skater type music because I adjusted my style accordingly. It was so great I got to wear huge baggy pants and band t-shirts that were oversized as well. I didn't really need to brush my hair and eventually it got all matted and dreadlocked. I purposefully made myself look as unattractive and messy as possible so I wouldn't have to deal with myself and my underlying issues. I thought I looked stylish and cool but looking back at photos now I can see I was just hiding from who I really wanted to be.

Who I really wanted to be was in shape and attractive. I wanted guys to ask me to dances and on dates. I wanted to be pretty and cute. I wanted to wear dresses and skirts and pretty jewelry and do my hair in the morning. I wanted to be popular. I didn't see this as possible for myself so instead I made fun of and shunned all those girls that acted and dressed that way. I would say they are all superficial and fake. They are too materialistic and shallow. In reality I was the one that was not expressing myself. I was crying for attention in any shape or form and the only way I knew how to do that was to be different.

I moved in with Tracy, my best friend from high school when I was 17 years old. Of course she was a twig and would have two or three guys she would be dating at any given time. I never had any boyfriends and would mostly choose to spend my Saturday nights with Ben and Jerry and sometimes even Mr. Daniels. I pretended like I didn't want a relationship and that guys were assholes. What I really wanted was someone to hold my hand and to share their experience of life with me. I certainly didn't know any guys my age that would be interested in such a thing considering the raging hormonal imbalances taking place in that period of life.

My life became a series of cleanses, diets, fasts, gym memberships and starting next Mondays. It consisted of popcorn diets, protein shakes, weight loss pills and every infomercial weight loss device under the sun. You name it I ordered it or at least considered ordering it.

Growing up in the 90 s wasn't easy for a girl who was always overweight. Especially when it was the heyday of being anorexically skinny and looking like a hanger for clothes. Every magazine you looked in, every TV show or movie you watched had some unrealistically skinny girl in it. Needless to say most of the time I wondered why I had to be such an ugly cow while everyone else got to have sex appeal and be beautiful.

This is probably when my problem with woman began. As I said before, I started judging, comparing, evaluating and pretty much hating any girl that was pretty and skinny. Underneath I secretly wished I was them. If I saw a girl that was overweight I felt at home, I knew she understood the pressures of the world. I knew that she'd understand that beauty isn't just about your physicality. Unfortunately in high school it kind of is. Who is going to ask someone who is overweight to a dance or out on a date? I always felt baffled when girls that were in high school who were even bigger than me had boyfriends. I just didn't understand it. The media had really done a great job of pulling the wool over my eyes. It brainwashed me so good that I spent the first 29 years of my life alone.

I thought every friend I'd ever had was prettier than me. All the girls I encountered in grade school, high school and beyond were so much cooler, stylish, and better than me. It seemed that every girl and woman had something that I didn't possess. I was by no means sexy or even attractive from my perspective. Every woman I saw on TV or in magazines was so lucky. They didn't have to deal with fat thighs, a huge ass or zits on their face. They didn't have to shop at cheap stores. Their parents took them to all the expensive clothing stores. I couldn't even begin to afford those stores let alone fit in the clothing sizes. Most girl's legs were as big as my arms at certain points in my life. The whole thing was a paradox. I wanted to be pretty and get attention but I also wanted to be unattractive and left alone. When you re unattractive (or at least when you think you re ugly) you devise ways to get attention and have people love you. You become loud or funny or rebellious and defiant. You make sure you re different and everyone knows it.

The funny thing is that I always knew that looks really don't have anything to do with anything. It's just a bonus that some people get in life but in no shape or form defines who you are or gauges your self-worth. It was so hard for me to understand that back then even though underneath everything I did. I was the one who chose to be unattractive and cut myself off from men and people. I made myself look so opposite of what my true self was. I compared myself to other girls who were probably doing the same thing. Women are really pieces of work. I dream of a world where we are not in competition with each other but instead love, value, and respect each other for each of our unique beauties and talents. How beautiful would it be if we were empowering one another instead of being caddy and jealous of each other.

I have learned infinite things from my so-called "ugly" days. One is that usually the only person that is judging you so harshly is you. Everyone else is too concerned judging themselves and their supposed shortcomings. I have also learned that EVERYONE truly is beautiful. Yes, it's a very corny thing to say but it really rings true for me. I can't say that I ever see ugly people. I take that back, people become ugly when they are thoughtless and selfish, however even those types have areas of beauty. We all have something that no one else has and the key to life is finding that thing and having it shine bright at its highest wattage.

I am now at a place in my life where I can say that I am beautiful. Sure I am not 6 foot tall super model, but who decided that that was the standard? We have all become so brain washed that we can't even think for ourselves or decide what WE think is beautiful or sexy. We do realize the fashion industry is controlled by a ton of gay men, right? SO basically women have been trying to adapt themselves to an image of what gay men think is attractive and hot? It's quite comical. I believe that we as a species are moving away from this and realizing what's real and what is not. Beautiful is so many different things and takes on so many traits. It's what somebody brings to situations and circumstances that is truly beautiful. It's handling a life challenge eloquently and gracefully. It's having a generous spirit and heart. It's being confident in who you are and what you bring. It's having the freedom to be yourself unabashedly. It is loving yourself and all your imperfections unconditionally. Its knowing that you are perfect right now and you won't be worth more when you lose twenty pounds or get your hair styled differently. Beauty is self-confidence and when you are being that, your distinct magnificence shines through. I think of all the time and energy I wasted on thinking of such superficial things and it makes me laugh. I forgive myself and also am eternally grateful that I can look in the mirror now and truly love the woman I see, (of course I still have my off days) but for the most part I see the things I love more than the things I do not. I focus on what's right with me instead of what's wrong.

CHAPTER 14

JAIL

There is nothing like being hauled off to a place that is one step short of the penitentiary, especially when you're a suburban white girl.

Speeding around the curb at 70 miles an hour in a 35 mile an hour zone is probably not the smartest idea, however when you've been drinking and popping Vicodins all night it seems like the only option when you are trying to get to community college on time.

"My Grandma didn't raise me this way," is all I could think of as I saw the bright lights of the school security vehicle pulling me over. The guard asked me for my license and then proceeded to call the police on me. I somehow managed to hide my intoxication and appear mature: at least I think that's what I looked like.

Before I knew it I was handcuffed inside a boring, sterile room inside the confines of the school. I had really done a great job at not revealing my non sobriety and using my charm to sweet talk the police officers, I gained their trust to at least remove the handcuffs. I was all types of foggy and hazy in my mind, I was trying to remember even getting in the car that morning. On the outside I was as calm as the Gulf of Mexico.

After about an hour an officer came in and told me I had a warrant out for my arrest from the City of Chicago. Apparently when I got caught shoplifting I had a court date I was supposed to show up to and didn't. I was supposed to go to that, who knew? So now I'd really done it. Not only was my grandma's car being taken away but they were going to transport me to jail in the city until someone bailed me out

To those of you who are uninformed and un-Chicagoans the city jail is probably the last place you'd ever want to go in your life besides hell. It's full of gang bangers, thieves, killers, sex offenders and drug addicts. I had heard about it up until this point but never thought I would have to worry about actually going there. Apparently I worried wrong.

The bus came to pick me up and I cannot recollect a time where I felt more out of place in my life. I boarded and they handcuffed me to a railing that was in the middle of the aisle. There were bars on the window and no ventilation. It was a hot summer day and I had made the bad move of wearing jeans and a heavy t-shirt, still self-conscious about my body at that point I suppose. We took off down the highway and arrived at our destination.

I can say that this was my first adult experience with knowing what it feels like to be a minority. I was about the only white person that existed by the time I actually got into the jail. Although I was a bit scared I found myself actually more curious about what events were going to transpire here. Here is an experience that I'm sure no one from home will ever have to go through and how I wound up here I'm still clueless about. When I think back about this time in my life one word comes to mind and that word is unconscious. I was asleep, the walking dead.

I was brought into a holding cell with a very interesting group of individuals, mostly prostitutes and drug addicts. One women's nose was bleeding constantly while another woman was scream praying in Spanish. The guards that we were dealing with were 300 pound dark skinned lesbian women who would yell at us if we even made a peep. A black woman I was sitting next to started talking to me and asked why I was there. I felt inclined to lie considering that compared to all these woman in here I was a sissy. I told her the truth however and she agreed to take me under her wing for the night. She had told me that she had been in and out of jail for most of her teen and adult life. She had kids and had to prostitute to make ends meet. I found it interesting that the lesson she was supposed to have learned by having kids so young actually ended up being her profession.

Processing of the inmates began and I as usual had no idea what to expect. This was a whole new world for me and one that I frankly wasn't too fond of at this point. We were told that we had to have mandatory blood and urine tests to make sure we do not have STDs. I was so pissed off because I was a virgin. I didn't need these tests. I had a decent upbringing. I didn't want to have babies when I was 16 and sleep with every other man that I come into contact with. I was clean, how did I get here!? Regardless of my resistance I had to have the tests which were completely invasive and uncomfortable. The process of getting to your cell is worse than just being in your cell.

Next the guards had to make sure that we weren't holding any drugs anywhere. They made us remove our belts and shoe laces if we had them on. (I finally realized where that pants hanging off the ass, no shoelace in shoes fashion statement came from.) I had an aha moment. The guard told me to strip naked and I became paralyzed. I had never been naked in front of anyone besides myself up until that point and I sure as hell wasn't going to get naked now. I started to cry and beg and the guards face showed no sign of sympathy or compassion. I felt like she may beat me up if I didn't comply. I complied and I was crying. She then directed me to "cough and squat." She had to make sure I wasn't holding any drugs in my private parts. What!? That thought never even occurred to me. I mean I had hidden drugs in my bra before but my vagina!? That's disgusting! The more this process went on I started having somewhat of a divine experience. I couldn't believe that I, an intelligent, loving, somewhat harmonious creature was being forced to be with all these criminals who felt more like animals than anything else.

So after the most humiliating moment of my life we were directed to wait in line for our cells. On the way we had to pass the male cells and were told not to make eye contact by any means. Of course I did not comply. I still have visions to this day of this one man staring me down like I was an unwrapped piece of candy. He must have been some type of sex offender because I could feel his filthy energy from a half a block away. I thought, "I need to learn to listen."

We finally arrived to the concrete box I would be sleeping in for the evening and I had to part ways with my Mother Hen. It was then I found out that this was no studio apt style living this was dorm room living. The guards opened up the five thousand pound door and told me to step inside. The first thing I saw upon entering was a giant wooden cross on the wall followed by seemingly hundreds of pictures of Jesus on the wall. Inside a woman who I cannot remember the name of now was praying in Spanish. I took a seat on the top bunk bed and thought about how interesting it was that I had ended up in a room with a Jesus freak. Although I wasn't religious and didn't understand the prayers the woman spoke, I felt protected, like I wound up in that cell for a reason. I placed my head on the pillow and surprisingly enjoyed a deep and restful sleep.

In the morning a friend came and dropped off bail money for me, they removed me from my cell, gave me back my things and set me free. Words cannot describe what it felt like to be outside inside in "normal" civilization again. I walked down the street toward the train and had a hundred different emotions flood over me. I could not believe that in the building I just left behind an entirely different world existed. One that us "straight-laced" people are not even privy to. A world where people's egos run the show and there is no way out. They are imprisoned physically but more so mentally, emotionally and spiritually. These people never had love, never had people to guide and direct their lives and thought that the only way they could make it was to hustle, steal, lie and kill. It was so sad. I felt that I had experienced the lowest vibration of human beings that exist. I felt helpless and hopeless for the way the world turns out for some people. I felt guilty that I was so privileged to have grown up in a nice suburb and although I didn't have a nuclear family I had a grandma and uncle that loved me. Why am I out here and those people in there? Why was I born a white woman and not a male minority? Does that even matter? I started questioning so many things about humanity, people, and life that day. It was one of the richest and most ignorance smashing experiences I could have ever had at such a young age. What I learned is appreciation for myself and respect for life. I learned that I wanted my life to go somewhere big so that I could help people feel more love. And most importantly I learned that most people on this planet are unconscious and need something to wake them up and make them aware that they could be so much more. I think about that security guard that pulled me over from time to time. If it wasn't for him and for that experience I may still be asleep or even worse asleep behind bars.

CHAPTER 15

SINKING IN CONCRETE

Have you ever had a moment of non- presence that today you can't even believe still happened? A time when you were so immersed in your thoughts you don't even remember an outside world existing? You know kind of like when you're driving on the highway for a half hour and suddenly arrive home with no recollection of how exactly that happened? Well I've had many such occasions and one in particular will stay with me to death and beyond.

Winter in Chicago is brutal, especially when you live close to the lake. It's icy, bitter and frigid and your skin starts to feel like a rubbery mask if you don't moisturize properly. One particular January I decided to take on a dog walking job in my neighborhood not because I loved dogs but because not one damn place in the city of Chicago felt like hiring me. I decided even though it wouldn't be anywhere near the type of money I'd be making at serving jobs, at least it was something. I had run fresh out of excuses for my landlord and was about to retreat to MSG flavored ramen noodles.

Every morning I would wake up around 8am to start my ritual of getting geared up for my routine route. I'd start with my thermal underwear followed by leg warmers, stretch pants, a hoody, at least three t shirts, mittens and gloves. I wore a purple coat that had a rip in it that I refused to get rid of, a couple pairs of socks, boots, a scarf and a hat. My route started at 9am but it would take me about an hour to get ready. Most days I wouldn't shower because what's the point when you're just going to get hot and sweaty from the thirty pounds of clothing you have on? At 8:45am I'd head out the door en route to peanut's house.

I can't exactly remember all the names of these little and big creatures I'd visit with Mon through Friday but one thing I do know is that they provided me with the right amount of affection, attention and annoyance I needed at that time in my life. The three hundred dollar paycheck I received every week wasn't bad considering I had been unemployed for what seemed to be decades.

I had about nine dogs all together on my route and it was quite the process to get in and out of the house, untying my boots and taking off some of my gear to go in, feed the dog and then return to the door to retie my boots and head outside in the frigid air for our religious thirty minute walk. Walking into some of these people's houses was quite interesting. I became convinced that you can easily judge a person by what their house looks like and how messy or dirty it is. You can also tell a lot about the owners based on the dog's personality. Keep in mind I never met any of the owners considering that the reason I was walking them is because they were at work. Each day I would walk in their houses and judge and access these people based on how many dishes were in the sink, If their toliet was clean and by the way their dogs treated me.

One dog in particular I should have known was going to cause me trouble. He was so opposite from my personality. It was clear that he was raised by some type of perfectionistic man. I was thinking probably a lawyer. This man's house was immaculate and always smelled like cleaning products and expensive whiskey. One day I looked in his closet to see if what I was suspected was true. All his suits were organized by color, labeled and hung in such a way that a wrinkle was impossible. There was never a smear or water stain on the mirror in the bathroom and never even one knife or fork in the sink. There was no dog hair anywhere and the dog's part of the house looked like a sterile hospital room. All in all I knew if I ever met this owner he would probably be upset that this sweaty bohemian child was walking his precious Ted.

Ted and I set out for our walk that day and walked all over the uptown area on Chicago's Northside. It had started to flurry out and I was losing feeling in my fingers even with mittens and gloves on. I would silently curse as I walked down the street because I was so freezing. I wondered how my life had gotten to this point. I was 27 years old and still walking dogs. Most of the people I knew were going for Master's degrees and at this point at least had some type of clue about their life's passion. Here I was sweaty, freezing, broke and walking some anal retentive gay man's dog around the block. It pissed me off.

I stayed heavy in thought about this and so much more for the duration of our thirty minute walk and realized I had to pee. I tied Ted up outside and went into the local coffee house. As I walked in I noticed that not one person was engaged in human to human contact. It was nothing but phones, computers, Ipods and electronic books. I got even more pissed off as I walked to the bathroom discussing with myself the problem with the world and the people in it. I peed, walked out and thought about the same thing getting progressively more annoyed. I untied Ted and continued walking towards his uptight owner's home.

I started to walk towards Ted's house and my mind started wandering in a way it had not before. Here is something along the lines of what it said. "I can't believe this shit, no one is connected anymore. No one cares about anyone anymore. We're all addicted to technology and can't even have a normal conversation. People can't even make eye contact with other people. Technology will eventually destroy us all. We're too dependent on it! Did u see that guy with his Ipod drawing pictures of bloody zombie people. He'll probably be a serial killer. Probably because he doesn't have parents that take care of him because they are too busy watching movies on their new plasma TV or having affairs with their secretaries. I can't believe these miserable human beings! We have lost our essence our source our beauty our truth, we are all afraid of ourselves and each other. We act powerless, we're more interested in finding out the score of the Bears game or watching crappy rap stars music videos than tending to ourselves, than nurturing our souls, than taking time to spend with our family members and friends than doing the things that really matter in life!!!" (insert scream and me pulling out my hair and choking Ted here.)

My mind is on a bloody rampage. I am so inside of my head that I am no longer looking to see if cars are coming when I cross the street, I'm not paying attention to if people are around me. I didn't even know if Ted was with me. I was just in automatic in my head robot thinking mode and then it happened.

I was sinking in concrete. I was shocked back to reality as I realized that I was waste deep in grey concrete in the middle of the Chicago street in the dead of winter. My first thought was, "How the hell did I manage this?" I mean not paying attention has definitely always been one of my defining characteristics, but this THIS is beyond belief! As I awoke from my mind slumber I surveyed the scene around me and saw that I had walked in between four horses that were blocking off the area and in the middle of a construction site that I had not even noticed due to my minds ramblings.

I hurriedly tried to pull myself out of the pit while Ted stood on the side, head nod and all, giving me a "you idiot" look. After all, Ted had noticed but I had not. As I tried to pull myself to the surface with my eight layers of clothing making me heavier than I already was four Mexican men came running shouting things in Spanish that I could not interpret. I got "Dios mio" but that's about it. By the time they had come I had managed to pull myself out, but not without losing my sock, my shoe and my dignity. One of the men grabbed a hose and started running toward me while passerbys were having mixed feelings. An old lady had a "poor girl" look on her face while a pre-pubescent teen was laughing hysterically. I couldn't help but laugh, it was so ridiculous. The Mexican man tried to hose me down but I declined seeing that it was negative 10 degrees out. I grabbed Ted and headed back to control freaks house with only one shoe. I thought I may have to have my toe amputated seeing as though the five minute walk felt like a five thousand mile journey.

When I returned I put Ted back in his sterile surroundings and searched for a sock in anal retentive's drawer. There was no way that I was going back in the arctic tundra without at least a sock. It was a twenty minute walk to my house. I took a pair of socks from the back of the drawer hoping he wouldn't notice and intending to replace it, gave Ted a treat and left.

As I walked back home, now aware that my whole schedule was about to be running at least an hour late, I reflected upon the event that had just occurred. I realized that all those thoughts I had had previous to the incident were just evidence that all those non present, in their heads, minds and electronic devices people were reflections of me.

CHAPTER 16

THE BEGINNING
OF THE SHIFT

My friend came into work a completely different person that day. We were both waiting tables at a pretty popular restaurant at the time. He was walking with more of a graceful stride and his eyes seemed clearer. I was standing cutting some bread to put into baskets and he came and told me about a weekend course he had just attended. I thought, "Oh God, has he been saved or inducted into a cult or something."

I remember in high school a bunch of students had gone on a weekend retreat and came back with some funky necklaces and a new found love for each other. The jocks loved the nerds, the preps loved the artsy kids and so on. I remember being highly annoyed. Probably more so that I had not attended the same weekend and wondered what miracle had taken place that all of a sudden switched everyone's perspective on one another. I felt left out.

My friend told me a little bit about the weekend he had attended and I couldn't quite grasp exactly what the hell he was talking about. He said something about, "living into your possibility" and "completing your past", it was all terminology I was not exactly hip to. It sounded interesting nonetheless. He invited me to a free introduction and a year passed before I actually got to one.

I was on the bus in the city on my way to this unknown organization that I had been told about at least a hundred times that year. It even ended up that I was taking the EL one day and a random man started talking to me about the course. I'm a pretty friendly person so I exchanged the small talk and then some deep talk as well. The man had asked me what exactly I wanted out of my life and I really didn't know how to respond besides saying the basic "things" most everybody wants. Money, a relationship, traveling, fun, etc.. He proceeded to tell me more about the course and I soon realized it was the same thing my friend had so devoutly shared over and over and over again.

I arrived at the seminar and was greeted by overly smiley faces: keep in mind at this point in my life I was mostly viewing the world as a cruel and unfriendly place. My friend and I were welcomed with multiple happy faces and everyone seemed almost overjoyed to meet me. They were all so delighted that I had decided to attend the introduction. I put my name and phone number on a piece of paper, they gave me a nametag and I walked into the room.

There were over a hundred people in the room and everyone seemed to be chatting and having a great time. I soon figured out that half the crowd had done the course and the other half had not. I took my seat and the evening began.

The speaker was a middle-aged man, who I thought could possibly be gay and was quite animated.

He started talking about what the course was about and what had happened in people's lives as a result of taking the course. He asked people to come to the microphone and share their experiences and inquired into what had "opened up" as a result of them attending the 3 and a half day course.

People started getting up to the mic quite freely and sharing about themselves and their lives. When people would get up to the mic they seemed calm and relaxed with giving out intimate details of their histories. I was shocked at how raw and candid it all was but mostly surprised at how REAL these people were being. The leader of the course explained a little more and continued to have people share about what the course had made available to them. I knew immediately that this is exactly what I had been looking for at this point in my life. Whatever that course leader had: the energy, liveliness, positivity and power: I wanted that and more. I wanted to break out of my old habits and out dated ways of thinking and that is exactly what the course was promising.

When it came time to register into the course, I put up a fight. It was 485 dollars (which looking back is dirt cheap for the value), however I only had 60 dollars in my bank account and rent was due soon. I was broke and once again money was holding me back from all the things I wanted to do in life. I had put off traveling for years due to this and once again something I really was yearning for was going to have to be put off until I had funds for it. Numerous people came up and talked to me and asked me similar questions. I just kept on saying, "I don't have the money for it right now." Finally one person I was interacting with asked me a question and said, "where else does that hold you back in life, not having money?" And just like that

I got it. I had gotten something huge for myself and wasn't even registered into the course yet. I thought about the way my life was going and how I hated it. There were so many things I wanted to be doing and money was the culprit for me not doing do. Deeper than that I saw that it wasn't in fact money it was me that was using that as an excuse. There was a lot of money to be made out there and I wasn't making it and furthermore I hated money and realized that I didn't even want any because of the misery it brought to the world! My friend offered to pay for half the course and I registered. I wasn't going to let money hold me back from one more thing I wanted to do. I was done with excuses. It was time to get serious.

It's funny because underneath everything I wanted to do the course just to prove to my friend that it wasn't as amazingly awesome as he said it was and that it really wasn't going to work on me. I mean my problems were really deep seeded and rooted and I was pretty positive that nothing was going to change that.... I was very wrong.

The weekend before the course was one of the worst of my life. I felt so trapped inside myself it was unbearable. There was a guy that I thought I was "in love" with at my work and I couldn't even speak to him I was so shy. I hated myself so much and wondered why it was so easy for other girls to be so flirty and cute with guys. When I liked a guy I would ignore or dodge him completely. I would even resort to being mean, bitchy and sarcastic at times. I would get nervous, stutter, and start turning red. It was very sixth grade. My biggest fear in life was being in a relationship. I was 25 at this time and had never been in a serious relationship. I had a minimal amount of sexual experience and felt very confronted about being intimate with a guy. Bottom line is that it scared the shit out of me and I decided early on that that was something I must avoid at all costs even though it was the thing I wanted most in my life.

All of this and more came bubbling to the surface and blaringly obvious a couple days before I entered into the course. I thought about what they had said when I registered which was, "the moment you register for the course, the course starts." Basically this implied that since you had created a future for yourself and committed to doing something to progress your life forward, you would start getting results before you even attended the weekend. What had happened in the weeks and day previous was that I would feel fearful or scared or worried but then I would question it. I hadn't been doing that up until this point, I had just accepted that this was what life had given me and this is what I had to live with. It was just my personality and I would always be shy and never be the woman I wanted to be. I started questioning the fear, questioning my personality and examining just why I got to be the way I was. I mean previous to this I had read many books and done many other forms of spiritual development and work on myself but I had never gotten so intimately tied to the question of "why am I the way I am?" I knew I had abandonment issues and that my Mother had passed away and all those other seemingly tragic events that had occurred but I kept on thinking why does that matter now. I felt like a balloon that was about to burst.

The weekend of the course I woke up late and arrived twenty minutes late. That was typical though. I dressed in jeans and a hoodie and and as usual didn't really give much bother to what I looked like. I walked into the room of about 130 people and sat in the back row with a hoodie over my head. I had made up my mind that I was not going to get up and talk for the whole weekend. I sat there for two hours wondering when the course was going to begin. People just kept on getting up to the mic and asking what the course was about and how the weekend was going to go and who was running the program and what can we expect and a bunch of other annoying questions. I just wanted the damn thing to start. After about two and a half hours I realized that it had started. A girl got up to the mic and started sharing intimately about the eating disorder she had had all her life and how she felt she was ugly and fat and wasn't good enough. I was looking at her baffled. In my eyes she was gorgeous and thin and I would have killed to look like her.

The stories went on and on. We took breaks every few hours and had meal breaks as well. People kept on getting up and sharing things they had not ever shared with anyone before. There was a common theme among everyone that got up and shared and that theme was that everybody felt inadequate or less than in some shape or form. Some people weren't pretty enough, while others weren't smart enough, others weren't lovable enough and others just felt like they never fit in anywhere. Every single person that went up to share had their version and we all started looking at exactly how our identities and personalities got constructed. It was mind altering when we saw that specific situations whether they had been big or small had profoundly impacted the way we were operating and living our lives.

So many things started coming to the surface for me. I was looking at the way I was raised and the things I made up about myself based on what kids in school used to say, or my teachers or my Grandma or anyone from my childhood would say. I started looking at specific situations and uncovered what ACTUALLY happened in them not what I had made up about it. Things started to get simpler and easier to decipher and life started becoming clearer and who I REALLY was started to emerge. I remember it all so vividly. It was as if I was slowly awaking from 25 year slumber. This was just on the first day. The course leader had told us that we would only get about 10 percent on the first day and the meat of the course was on Sunday. That was the day we would blow it all open. It was only Friday.

I arrived Saturday and I was on time and honestly I do not have much recollection of that day because I was still in the inquiry of the previous day. They had given us homework to do and I can't recall it specifically but what I do know for sure is that it had something to do with sharing yourself with someone and why you were doing the course you were doing. Saturday was really just expanding and digging a little deeper than the previous day. People kept sharing about their life stories and experiences and we all saw things about ourselves we had not seen before. We had homework that night too.

Sunday. Who would have thought that one day or one conversation could have such an effect on your life? Little did I know that when I walked in that day I would be forever changed...for the better. My view of everything in my life up until that point shifted so dramatically it was utterly surreal. All the things I thought about myself and who I thought myself to be were changed. The way I viewed people and the seemingly stupid things they do changed.

All different ages and walks of life attended the course and every single one of us got it to varying degrees. I finally saw that I was in creative control of my life and I had the power to shift and transform anything I wanted. It was unchartered territory. I got that fear is something I wasn't going to let run me anymore and that I actually would be able to manifest all those things I had always thought were unobtainable. I forgave the people who had all shaped who I was up until that point. I thanked them as well. I was proud to be a person that wanted to grow and expand themselves at the age of 25. I still had friends that were acting like they were 16 at that point. I attribute a lot of my life to having done that course. Without it I don't know where I would be right now. I feel that I am ten years ahead of myself and that my growth accelerated. I share the course with pretty much anyone I come into contact with. It is meant for all human beings and definitely can and is transforming the world one person at a time.

CHAPTER 17

DONTI

In my eyes, my Grandmother was one of the coolest women to ever walk the face of planet earth. I'm sure other people who are not related would agree. I loved her so much that I am resisting writing a chapter about her considering I will want to go on for hours. Similar, to my Mother, I learned infinite things from her and also learned things I wish I wouldn't have.

As I ve said before, my Mother came in and out of the picture, but after second grade I pretty much consistently lived with my Grandma and Uncle. My Mother would visit often. For some reason when she was pushing me around in a grocery cart one day I started calling her Dante. Not sure what that name was supposed to mean but it stuck for her entire life.

Dante was definitely like a Mother to me and sometimes was more so than my real Mother. She always made sure I had food and clothes and most importantly love. My whole childhood she went back and forth from being extremely overweight to moderately. Looking back I can see that she was more overweight during more trying times in her life. Much like everyone else in the family there was a definite lack of self-love and compassion going on. My Grandfather had passed away when I was only three years old so I can't remember him quite that well. I've been told that I loved him dearly and there are many pictures to prove it. We were both Scorpios and born one day a part so how could I not? He had come home from work and complained of a shooting pain in his left arm, they took him to the hospital and he was gone the next morning. He had died of a heart attack. No signs, no warning, just gone. This obviously had a severe and profound impact on my family. Death is never easy but it's a little bit tougher when it comes so unexpectedly.

If there is one word I would use to describe my Grandma it would be fun. She was always jovial and would talk to anyone at any time. It appeared that she had no prejudices or judgements about people. She just wanted people to get along and love each other. After I saw the movie Titanic, the character the unsinkable Molly Brown kind of reminded me of her. She would never treat anyone condescendingly. It felt as though in her world equality always prevailed.

I loved my Grandma more than any human being I have ever encountered, I would attribute a large portion of my personality to her influence. I will talk to anyone, anywhere at any time. Of course I am judgmental as we all can be at times, however I do question my judgments due to her guidance.

Many people called her a gypsy and it was easy to see why given the way she dressed. She would wear long flowey outfits with dangly sparkly earrings and cake on the make-up. I remember getting so embarrassed of her from time to time. She really didn't give a shit what anybody thought of her, which was very difficult to deal with when I was a teenager.

She would go into stores and just try on clothes in the middle of the aisle instead of going into the dressing room. She seemed to make up her own rules for things which had some people love her and others get highly annoyed with her. She followed her own life plan not the pre-determined one.

The lessons I learned from My Grandma are innumerable. She was the one that taught me how to be my own person and not follow the masses. She did what made her happy unapologetically. She didn't care who thought she was weird or bizarre. I know sometimes she felt like she was a stranger on this planet, like she didn't belong. I was blessed to be raised by someone who had a fun and free spirited way of looking at life.

On the opposite end of the spectrum her free spiritedness and carefree nature is now something I have to balance out a bit. Sometimes she would frivously spend money she didn't have or we would overeat and overindulge in food. I believe that was her way of coping with the empty spot my Grandfather had left in her heart.

When my Grandma passed away she was 81, it was one of the hardest and most surreal days of my life. I didn't want to believe it was happening and still have trouble even processing it. After almost five years I still haven't completely gotten over it and I probably never will. She had congestive heart failure and was in and out of the intensive care unit for years. Every time she was in the hospital I had thought that was it. She trudged on though and made it through. She lived with my Uncle and he took care of her, I would visit occasionally. I still have a lot of guilt and resentment toward myself for not being more loving to her in her last years. I would get so frustrated that she was so slow with walking or she would need help taking a shower. I had no patience for her state of mind and state of health. There were times that I was downright mean to her and it makes me so sad to think I was capable of being that way. I still have to consciously forgive myself every now and then.

I am so thankful to have had a woman in my life who taught me to have a strong sense of self. She taught me how to live off the beaten path and to be creative and spontaneous. She showed me that love is the way and that life is just a game. The way she loved me was like no other. She always made me feel special and like I was the most interesting person in the world. She wanted to be like me as I got older. If I got a cool pair of shoes the next time I would come over she would have the same ones. She admired me and loved the way I lived my life which probably seemed fearless to her.

I miss Dante so much and am sad that she is not here with me on this earthly plane anymore, however I know she is my angel and watches guides and protects me along with my Grandfather and my Mother.

CHAPTER 18

TOOTH FAIRY

The way he walked turned me on. There was nothing particularly intriguing about him besides his perfect posture, endless tattoos and "Don't fuck with me attitude." The day he walked in for an interview I said goodbye to my sanity and hello to my obsessive, lusty and persistent thoughts. His holey Chuck Taylors and skin tight black pants would occupy my interior landscape for hours on end. It certainly made my mindless job of filling up nut bins a lot more exciting.

I had worked at a popular health food store for a little over a year and had had a crush on pretty much every living and breathing man that worked there. I never did anything about it though because of my phobic shyness and if someone asked me out I would just ignore it or act like it wasn't happening. I decided living in a fantasy world suited me much better so that's just what I did. Fantasy is waaay better than reality. Reality means having conversations with men and actually spending time with them, learning about them and their lives, meeting their families and dealing with their emotional baggage and so on and so on and so on. Sounded like a whole lot of work and a job that I was not up to. I mean I have to deal with all my emotional baggage as well. All of it is just way too heavy. Fantasy better.

I didn't want to deal with my issues or face myself so I used fantasy and obsession as a way to escape and relieve some of the pain of really wanting to be in an intimate and loving relationship but not being able to. It was my temporary vacation and permanent retreat for years.

My friend nicknamed him tooth fairy, his real name was Brad and he was a Scorpio. We came up with the name so we could speak in code if I called her from work to obsess over the details of our encounters that day which were usually pretty lackluster. Not sure why she named him this but I think it was because of his elusiveness and mysteriousness.

Before we getter any further if you're waiting for some type of steamy sex scene or anything grand you're not going to get it. The most you'll probably get is a short in depth convo but that's about it and to me that was enough.

Tooth fairy would walk around the aisles of the store with his chest pumped out and his head cocked back just a little further than everyone else. He dripped of testosterone and awoke some type of primal carnal part of me I didn't know existed. I would watch him talk to customers and win them over with his gift of gab and charming smile. That was another thing that had me hooked, the way he interacted with people seemed so genuine and heart-felt. He was a dirty punk rock kid with a missing tooth but on the inside he was an enlightened soul crying for attention and love. His ego overshadowed his beautiful white light because that what it does, it hides the truth. It was all very dramatic.

When I met him I knew he was a Scorpio (one of me) upon eye contact. His sex appeal was undeniably obvious and he seemed to be oozing of it. I knew that he had just moved from Oregon but came to find that he was originally from Chicago. It was so perfect because his section was right next to mine. All the hot men used to come into the room that I was working in to visit me. At first I thought it was because they all liked me but once I snapped out of my daydreams I came to find that it was probably more likely because I had food all the time.

Every word that this guy said to me I made meaning out of, it was like witnessing myself being a 12 year old giggly bashful girl again and again. I couldn't even stand in the same space with him without starting to sweat and turn red. He was so dominating and overwhelming. We would have conversations about random things having to do with a Scorpios favorite topic: life. We would talk about crystals and aliens and things of that sort. This made me think we were soul mates, but then again any guy who has had any similar interests to me for the greater part of my life I thought was my soul mate.

I never really knew for sure whether or not Brad would have gone for me. I would fantasize for hours on end about how he was secretly in love with me and create scenarios in my mind of him and I making out in the coolers at work. I would make up that when he was being cold to me that it was just his way of telling me that he is interested. Apparently, I related to him as though he was a grade school boy. I thought that he was hiding his feelings for me just like I was hiding mine. Anytime I would even come in close contact with him or see him walking down the aisle or hall toward me I would pray that he could not read my mind and all the sexually aggressive thoughts I was thinking about him.

My constant preoccupation with him completely took me out of the game of life. I used fantasy as a distraction to getting what I wanted in real time life. I noticed that I do this in many areas of my life. I create and make up fake scenarios and scenes that have me avoid getting what I actually want. I'm sure this is a common coping mechanism for a lot of people, especially women. I wasted a lot of my time and life fantasizing and thinking about ideas, relationship and things that never came into fruition mostly because I didn't take any action on any of them. I found out that taking action will more likely than not get me the thing I wish to possess or that thing I desire. The moment I started taking just a little bit of action in my life things started manifesting. Fantasy is just a means to distract you from getting the things you really want.

CHAPTER 19

AWKWARD YET HONEST

When men started showing interest in me I would attempt to flirt or be cute and trust me the first hundred times were disastrous. I would shake, turn red, sweat and shy away, but I trudged on. I started purposely trying to talk to more straight men in the workplace and consciously chose certain men that I would talk about intimate (not sexual) things with. I came to find that men trusted me and even more respected me. I actually started loving men and getting how wonderful and incredible they are. I saw that they provide so much to woman and that I wanted to start focusing on the positive instead of the negative. This also had me do the same with myself...focus on what's great and beautiful about me instead of what's wrong.

The first actual "date" I went on was in my late twenties. There had been times that I "hung" out with guys by myself but I never considered them actual dates. The first date I went on was with a co-worker who was moving out of state two days later, this obviously made it a little easier for me. I figured I needed the practice and he was perfect for that. I had found him very cute for the whole time I worked there and he had passed hints to me many times that he thought the same about me, I would just usually ignore them though. One of the last days before his last day working there he came in the back and asked me out and I got extremely flustered to the point of pretending that I didn't hear the question. I just stood there doing something else making no eye contact. He left the room and I exhaled.

Later on that day I found him in one of the aisles at work, mustered up the courage and marched right up to him and gave him my number and told him to call me. For those of you with a fear of public speaking this would have been the equivalent of delivering a speech to a fully packed Madison Square Garden.

Two days later we made plans through text and he picked me up at my place around 8pm. This was my first actual date with someone and I couldn't believe I was actually doing it. The car ride to the bar we went to was a very short distance thank god because the conversation in the car was pretty awkward.

When we arrived at the bar we got a table and I noticed that he had somehow managed to spray some cologne on him without me seeing on the way from the car to the bar. We sat at the table and I just tried to pretend like he was a gay man. It only worked for so long until he started complimenting me. I started sweating profusely and hoping and praying that he couldn't see. And then something happened. I decided to spill the beans and call myself out. I started telling him how I was terrified of men and that this was the first actual date I had ever been on. I told him what was happening to me physically and that he was actually in the process of helping bust through my biggest fear. This turned into an amazing conversation where he ended up opening up to me about his fears and about his life and stuff that he deals with. I found that he was nothing like I suspected. I had it that he was just some typical Italian guy from a typical Chicago neighborhood and I found that he was funny, intelligent and much more educated than I had originally suspected. The night ended up being great. But then...

I got a little bit ahead of myself with the fear facing and after being a few beers in when he was dropping me off at home I decided to invite him up. I had never done anything like that. I mean I had definitely ended up in beds and people had ended up in mine after drunken nights but I had never fully and consciously invited someone up on purpose. He obviously accepted the invitation with open arms.

When we got into my apt my roommate was sleeping, so we crept past his room into my room. I found him to be very sexy and wanted more than anything to be the type of woman that could have unemotional and animalistic sex. Remember at this point I was still virgin, although the only one that knew that was me because I lied to all my friends about my sexual encounters so they wouldn't think I was a loser or a prude. All in all in was too much too fast. I took his shirt off and started giving him a massage. Things escalated fast and before I knew it all our clothes were off and he was ready to go. I knew he hadn't even given a thought to the evening ending like this and he was pleasantly surprised.

He started approaching my sacred portal and everything just stopped, he tried to get in and couldn't. My body got so tight and I was so disgusted with myself that I was so desperate to be sexually intimate with someone that I would just let some guy I didn't really even know at all take my virginity.

Needless to say he felt like a failure and got a little upset. I can't even remember if he relieved himself. What I do know is he layed down next to me and I tried to snuggle him. He told me he had to go. He was probably really embarrassed looking back.

I'm not exactly sure what the point of this little story is however I felt the need to include it because it really was a turning point for me. It had me see for the first time that it was actually possible for me to be myself and still be attractive. It showed me that actually the only time someone is truly attractive is when they are being themselves with no pretenses and no fakeness. The hottest thing in life is confidence and letting your walls down. We tend to think that we need to put on a façade to attract the perfect mate or we need to pretend to be somebody that we're not. These are the things that push people away and never have us find true love. In order to have what we really want in our lives we have to be authentic and honest and most importantly be willing and ready to call ourselves on our bullshit.

CHAPTER 20

MEETING MATTHEW

There is nothing that can prepare you for meeting the love of your life. I had decided to try the online dating scene because meeting someone organically just wasn't quite working out. At this point I was still in terror land over even going on a date. It just always all seemed so fake to me. It's like let's just meet up and see if we think we want to sleep together. That's what it always felt like to me and that's probably why I avoided it. For years I thought men were just not interested in me, I mean there was way too much competition out there. Pretty girls are a dime a dozen. I assumed that in order to be in a relationship you had to be a classic beauty. You had to look like the girls on the covers of magazines. For years I had been trying to lose thirty pounds so I could then meet the love of my life. I needed to be prepared and beautiful. That why it made perfect sense that I met the love of my life when I was at my heaviest point.

My friend from work had set up an online dating account for me on a free website. I took it completely as a joke in the beginning and made a fake profile. I was infamous for not taking things seriously especially of that nature. I let the profile sit there for about a year before I started genuinely taking interest. I had still not met anyone and decided that online dating would have to be the way to go. My friend helped me legitimize my profile with true things about myself. We found a few semi cute pictures and put them up. This in and of itself was very confronting for me considering my major sensitivity around my looks. Despite my fear, I trudged on. Most of the responses I got were either silly, gross or just straight up rude. I guess what can you expect nowadays especially with a free website? I didn't really get any serious inquiries and again left it up for about a year and never even checked it once.

A year passed again and I was still boy friendless. I decided to log on one last time before I closed out the account just for entertainment purposes. At this point I had given up the notion that the relationship I wanted even existed, I was incredibly unattached and finally had come to terms with that I could lead a happy life on my own. And that's when it happened.

I logged on and got a message from Matthew that said, "Hey, I see that we have a lot of things in common. I am feeling a connection after reading your profile. By the way your favorite band is also mine by light years. Would love to talk." It was the first really serious response I got and I was struck by how cute the guy was. I was even more struck by his manners and respectability. Scared shitless I responded back with a time to talk. You have to understand this was a HUGE step for me. My phobia was slowly melting into a high level of anxiety. Very slowly.

The first time I ever spoke with Matthew it was about ten minutes if even. I was walking into work and took solace in the fact that I would only be available for a very short period of time for our first vocal encounter. I called my friend and shared my extreme fear with her and she encouraged and supported me and told me how great I was. I know for quite a few of you out there relationship and dating are quite a normal thing, for some of you a bit too normal. I would like you to identify and imagine your worst fear whether it be heights, spiders or any other thing we can come up with. Apply this to me and being in a relationship. It seemed completely incomprehensible to me and was utterly the most terrifying thing I could think of, however I wanted to challenge myself to the max so I called him.

"Hello?," he didn't sound too enthusiastic or excited as I would come to find is just Matthews natural way of expressing himself. I spoke shakingly and introduced myself and told him where I worked which at the time was a widely known health food store. We somehow got on the subject of holistic health, supplements and his Father's illness. We hung up ten minutes later. Instant connection.

The next time we spoke I was walking home from downtown Chicago all the way to the Northside. I had attended a lecture and planned a call with him purposefully knowing that the walk home would be at least two hours. Once again he answered quite unenthused and we immediately started sharing about our lives. It just felt like we had so much to say to each other. There was never any hesitation or lack of conversation. It flowed effortlessly like a waterfall into a river. It was stream of consciousness bouncing back and forth. Before I knew it I had arrived at my front door over two hours later. It had felt like five minutes. It seemed that time didn't exist and all there was was us and our conversation. I am convinced that something divine was happening. We covered most territories from childhood to past relationships to belief systems to secret hope and fears. After a five hour conversation that seemed like ten minutes we decided to talk again.

The next few times we talked the conversation was the same, effortless, flowing and never a lack of material. I clocked one of our conversations at a little over six hours. We told each other things we had never shared with other people before, we laughed and basked in the knowingness of each other even though we had not ever physically met. We exchanged phone calls and constant text messages for the next month or so. It felt just like the movies and I didn't even have time to believe it was actually happening. I didn't get too excited because we had not met each other in physical reality yet. I was convinced one of us wouldn't find the other attractive, there had to be some kind of catch here this was too good to be true. I also considered that this was my first time being in love and it was about his third. I knew a lot of naivety could be coming from my end. After our month of talking on the phone and sending each other emails we planned a date to meet and now I was really terrified. It's no problem sharing hopes, fears and dreams over the phone. In person face to face is a bit different. Terrifying.

The day I knew I was going to meet him seems surreal to me now that I think back. I was in massage school at the time and completely un-present in school all day. He had decided to drive to the city to meet me after he got off of work. Driving to Chicago from the suburbs at 5 in the evening is more frustrating than a trigonometry equation. He was willing to do it which was admirable in my book. I had no idea what to wear and all day long was feeding myself positive self-talk and motivation. I was offering myself empowering dialogue throughout the day and into the early and late afternoon. I got home from school and got dressed. I opted to just be myself and dress comfortably and casually as I always did.

I headed out to the location we were meeting at which was a few blocks from my apartment right on Lake Michigan. It was the middle of winter and the air was biting. I had a two sizes too big down comforter of a coat on and set out onto the icy sidewalk. I walked slowly and intentionally and continued to dowse myself with positive feedback. The whole time I was walking I kept thinking, " Holy shit I am about to meet my soul mate!" Usually at this point I would have dialed a friend and vented about my hopeless fear however I chose to talk to myself and tried to get excited despite my awful nerves.

I remember walking into the store and meeting him in semi slow motion. I was so concerned we wouldn't find each other attractive. He had texted me to let me know where he was in the store. I walked in and rounded the corner and saw him standing in the aisle he said he would be in. The first thing I noticed was how sparkly his eyes were, which in retrospect could have just been the ambient lighting from the store. I have a tendency for dramatics as previously stated. Looking back I could see him being my reflection although at the time my nerves wouldn't allow me to pay attention to such a thing. He was a little taller than me and I found him to be adorable. I wondered so intensely what his initial impression of me was? We gave each other a knowing hug and proceeded to get some dinner and checkout. I don't even know how I made it through all that without passing out. It felt as though something was guiding and protecting me from my fear. I do believe in angels and I believe they were helping me out hugely that night.

We ate dinner and it was evident that both of us were nervous although we gave our Oscar award winning best performances pretending that we weren't. Neither of us really grasped who the other was at that point. We had no idea that we would endure the next couple years together, all the things we would learn and people we would lose. We were at the beginning of one of the most if not THE most transformative points of our lives. We balanced. What I had he lacked and vice versa. It was like we were the same person but with many fundamental opposite end of the spectrum differences. Someone at work had mentioned twin flames quite a few times for about a month before I met Matthew. I never knew what that was until he mentioned it. I started obsessively researching it and came to discover that the reason I never had a relationship was because I never knew what I wanted. The only reason we don't get what we want in life is because we are not clear with our intentions and our hearts desires. We have ideas but not clear cut vision. We need 20/20 crystal clear vision. Once I started researching twin flames I had for the first time in my life discovered what I wanted out of my one and only relationship I was going to manifest. We went for a couple beers after dinner and then he dropped me off at home. He got out of the car and came around to my side and gave me a peck which I resisted. Fear; Pure fear.

I called my friend after Matthew had pulled off into the distance. I decided to take a walk around the neighborhood while talking to him. He interrogated me about the date and my feelings and his attractiveness level and everything. He knew of my fear well and was highly impressed that I had finally gotten into action around finding the "one." I wasn't sure at that point exactly what I thought but knew he was it in my heart. There is no way to articulate it besides saying it was a knowing. Having knowing feelings are so right brained they are super easy to resist, however this is where the truth and the spice of life truly exists. We are so left brain logic ruled that a lot of freedom, creativity and happiness gets removed from our lives. My heart knew it my mind didn't and I still deal with that to this day sometimes. My heart knows and it always will.

The second time we met Matthew took the train down to the city and we went for dinner and a beer again. We still didn't run out of dialogue and it was a bit more comfortable this time. We ended up getting quite buzzed or at least I did and he decided to bring out a poem he had written asking me to be his girlfriend. I freaked out and told him I wasn't ready and I was just starting to date and I ran to the bathroom. I came back to the table and then changed my mind. I must have occurred as mentally challenged at this point. I hadn't really shared the extent and depth of my fear with him at this point. Needless to say he was very confused and I was still resisting the whole thing. We got in a cab to take him back to the train station because he had to catch the last train back to the suburbs, by this point I was pretty drunk and leaning into his lap in the taxi. I walked him into the station to drop him off at the train and we still had a few minutes before the train departed. We stood in the lobby and he backed me up into a post and attempted to kiss me a few times and I fought back with every attempt. He got upset that I would not reciprocate after just agreeing to date him. He headed to get on the train and I ran after him apologizing profusely. Before he went to get on the train I attempted to kiss him and instead ended up licking his chin, it was quite messy but at least I had showed that I really did care.

He boarded the train and I felt so sad and thought I had blown it. I wanted to text him but couldn't because my phone was dead. I got in a cab and took it back to my house about fifteen minutes away. It felt like the longest ride of my life. I so badly wondered what he was thinking. Finally I arrived back home and with lightning speed got upstairs and charged my phone up. I texted him and apologized for my creepy and confusing behavior. He was pretty forgiving. I then decided in my buzzed state to just go with my gut, and go with my heart and I texted him I love you. He responded with you love me? And I said yes. I know on his end he was confused but he also understood at the same time. After 29 years I had finally found who I had been searching for my whole life, my other half, my twin flame, my ultimate mirror. I had manifested the most sacred and transformationally challenging relationship that exists. I had found my twin flame.

And now almost three years later, we continue to grow and learn from each other daily. The things we find most frustrating are usually the things that we can identify in ourselves. I believe a lot of people give up on each other if things are not going their way. My generation especially seems like they have become weak. It seems that marriage has lost its sacredness and it is something that is not viewed as permanent anymore. When you find someone you really love, you always have to remember to stay in your heart and not your head. Your mind will sabotage a great thing, it will tell you lies and make you believe that things are harder than they actually are. It will convince you that you do not love someone you really do. It will tell you to run when your heart tells you to stay. If you listen to your heart you will always have happiness in your relationship. If you openly communicate, especially about those things that are hardest to communicate you can know nothing but happiness, intimacy and trust.

For Matthew and I, it feels like we have always been together and is sometimes hard to remember what life was like without each other. It is the one thing I waited my whole life for and has been one of the most rewarding experiences I could have ever asked for. Being in a relationship is one of life's greatest gifts and challenges. It is a wonderful gift to grow, experience and walk through life with another. To watch each other grow, learn and transform in to new and more highly expressed individuals. It is amazing to be that person who gets to know the other more closely than anyone else in their life. You learn how to let things go, how to have forgiveness and compassion, how to truly love another and to accept someone unconditionally for everything they are and more importantly everything they are not.

CHAPTER 21

RESISTANCE TO THE DISTURBANCE, IS THE DISTURBANCE

The first time I met Matthew's Father I was struck by how handsome he was being that he was all skin and bones. He had salt and pepper hair, big brown eyes, a darker northern Mexican skin tone and long eyelashes. Even more he had an unwavering spirit, the most charming smile you've ever seen and the strength of ten warriors. It was clear where my boyfriend Matthew had acquired his good looks and worldly knowledge from. Gary had been diagnosed with ALS aka Lou Gehrig's disease ten years previous by the time I had first met him.

To those of you unacquainted with this disease, let me give you little background. I too had no clue what it was until I experienced it. I had certainly heard of it and knew it had to do with some baseball player from decades ago but that's about it.

ALS is the worst disease that exists in my opinion or at least the worst thing I have personally encountered in my life thus far. Basically without getting too technical the motor neurons in your brain stop functioning so they can no longer send signals to your muscles to move therefore causing paralysis. For some people it starts in their upper body and others the lower body. Either way you cut it, all the muscles eventually stop functioning leading to suffocation or choking in most cases. I know I don't normally think of using muscles when I'm breathing or eating but we are all using them all the time. Life expectancy for this disease is 2 to 5 years depending on the case.

Gary was five years past the life expectancy when I met him and I knew he wouldn't be in my life for much longer. I felt a soul connection when I met him though. He was very evolved and interested in the mystical and esoteric teachings of different teachers and philosophers. I could relate and he reminded me a lot of my late Mother. Unfortunately, at the time I met him he had lost a lot of his speaking skills. It was still possible to understand him but I had to listen very carefully and watch him get frustrated when he couldn't get his point across.

There is something that is so sacred about watching someone go through the process of dying. He maintained the whole time that he knew him that he was going to make it, but we all could see that that most likely wasn't going to happen. The disease is brutal and really doesn't offer any relief for its victim. We had many conversations about why he thought this was happening to him and I remember one conversation specifically where we both came to the conclusion that it was lack of self-love.

I believe that disease is a mental and emotional problem. That idea that I have read in numerous texts resonates with me one hundred percent. As I said earlier, I have had personal experience with this as well. I believe that when you don't love yourself and you have obsessive self-defeating thoughts that you can actually destroy your immune system and let disease in. You tap in to a vibration that sometimes is not all that high.

Watching Gary go through his process was one of the most heart-breaking yet enlightening and eye opening experiences I have had in my life. It would take him an hour to eat something that would take a healthy person fifteen minutes. He devised all types of ways to do things that weren't easy for him anymore. He found a way to wrap his paralyzed hands around a beer bottle to drink it. He found a way to take pills that didn't so easily slide down his throat anymore. Watching someone who wanted to live so much made it hard to look at people who have no value for their lives. Yet still, I believe everyone is getting what will evolve their souls to the highest possible level.

There was another part of me that viewed him as very prideful and resistant. I had the underlying feeling that he had regretted and withheld a lot of things in his lifetime. I had the feeling that he had attracted this illness to himself through his self-hatred, anger and constant negative thinking about himself. He never fully accepted that he had the disease and that could have possibly helped him. But hey what do I know? You never know what anything is like until you experience that thing for yourself. It just seemed that if he would of surrendered he wouldn't have suffered so much, but also everything is as is should be.

Watching Matthew and his Mom, Veronica go through this was a whole other layer. There were just so many layers to the situation. Everyone was just suffering so much, including me even though I never really said anything about it. Matthew is an only child and his parents seemed to be some of the best you could find, especially these days. They nurtured, loved and took time with him. They were a very close unit on many levels. Matthew's Dad was his best friend and Veronica his soul mate. He was a fix it all guy. One artifact that he left behind was his tool belt which Matthew will never give up. I never got to know him when he was well which felt like total robbery to me.

The year that I got to know Gary and watch his struggle was one of the most stressful, rewarding and worthwhile years of my life. Matthew had so much emotional stuff going on around it that he sometimes took it out on me. Veronica ended up retiring from her job of 25 years to take care of him full time. She ended up having no life and not being able to go anywhere. Gary would not go out anywhere because of his self-consciousness. He would make comments like, "I don't need to go anywhere, everything is within." This kind of annoyed me but in retrospect I now understand what he was saying. It seems that most of us seek external things to achieve happiness. I know for myself that I've always thought the more places I travel to and the more people I meet the happier my life will be. If I have things I want, enough money and cool friends then I will be happy. If I find my soul mate and am at my perfect weight then I'll be happy. Well Gary taught me that happiness is a choice and it is something that is within. I'm not quite sure he even knew this is what he was teaching me but he was.

I learned that not loving myself and being self-destructive is a really bad idea. I learned that not appreciating the things that I have is even worse. I became more present to the things I often take for granted like taking a shower, eating dinner, or driving a car. I discovered that there is a veil that we are all living under. It seems that there are two different worlds going on her on planet earth. One of those worlds is unconscious and all our routines and habits are robotic and premeditated. The other one is a slower, more graceful appreciative and loving existence where we take time to smell the flowers, create time to be with the people we love and appreciate and savor and relish every moment. Watching someone die really gets you present to life and how incredible this journey we have been given is. It has you reevaluate your priorities and plans. It makes you realize if not NOW, when?

CHAPTER 22

MY PERSONAL TRUTH

Life is an incredible journey that many of us take for granted and even end up hating a lot of the time. The pain, misery, loneliness, jealousy, anger and sadness can be a lot to handle at times and even become unbearable. All of these emotions come from the same place and that is fear. These are the times that we need to step back and reevaluate ourselves and our situation. We need to choose to move past those things that stop us most and to choose what we have and what we have been given. Live in love and acceptance instead of fear and resistance.

Life is beautiful. Life is great. You can have anything you want when you change your mind to change your mind. We have so much creative control and can turn any seemingly tragic event into an opportunity for growth. The hardest things in life are the ones that bring us closer to being the highest expression of ourselves...if you so choose. The tragic things in life if not dealt with in a healthy way can bring you even farther away from your light if you let them. It's all a choice. There is no truth that anyone will ever know for sure. If you choose an empowered conscious capable and responsible way of living you will have empowered conscious capable and responsible things coming into your life. If you choose to be a victim you will have more things to be a victim about. If you complain you will attract more things to complain about and so on and so on.

It is truly a privilege to be a human being. As the quote goes, "we are spiritual beings having a human experience." This is just an experience, kind of like a vacation from who we really are. And who are we? I believe we are souls and spirits who have unlimited capacities. Our inner consciousness: the same as outer space. We are vast, empty and able to be filled with whatever we deem possible for ourselves. If we believe that we can have anything we want then anything we want is what we will have. You want to change the world, start at home. The time has come to remember who we are and not just a few of us, all of us. Transformation and evolution are not just for a select elite few anymore. Too many of us have been working our asses off and displaying acts of courage that you wouldn't believe so that everyone can come along with us. It is time to grow, evolve, learn and experience what being a human being is all about. Utopian societies can and will exist. A place where suffering has ended, war is extinct and communication is the norm. A place where we do not judge each other harshly. We are all free to be who we want to be which divine and unique expressions of self. We are the Creator, we believe that the creator is some entity outside of us but we are the creators. We're all pieces of energy of one eternal source that have been split into seven billion different pieces creating an illusion that we are all islands. Don't fall for it. All of us are of the same lineage. We are all brothers and sisters. No one is innately better or smarter than anyone else. We are trapped in an illusion and consistently continue to believe the illusion.

I have come to find that I am just like everyone else, I am not special or extraordinary on my own. All people, all humans, both genders, all races, all religions, all belief systems. We are all beautiful and unique and none of us are any different from each other. We all have access to the same thing. We all can tap into our natural capacity blossom into our true selves.

Life is such an awesome experience. Instead of just letting it happen quite a few of us resist it and live our day to day lives in fear. Thinking about how we go through each decade of our lives and learn and grow and expand and learn to express ourselves in new exciting ways is so amazing. What mattered to me when I'm 20 will not have any relevance when I'm 30 just like when I turn 50 what matters to me today won't even be on my radar. At any point in time we may stop and think that "now we have it all figured out." This happens to me quite often. I look at the way I used to be and then remind myself that I am so happy I am not like that anymore. I get excited that I have learned so much and sometimes think, "What else is there to learn?" I mean I understand quite a few of the laws of the universe, I've read just about every self-help book under the sun, done multiple courses, distinguished why I am the way I am, found out that I'm judgmental and non-accepting, What else could there possibly be to learn!? It never ends. We are all bottomless pits of self-discovery and expansion. We will never be done growing and never arrive at that perfect place. Even if in this lifetime you reach some type of enlightenment as we understand it you will still be growing inside of that.

We are living inside an illusion and consistently continue to believe the illusion. We feel limited and inadequate when what we really are is unlimited and necessary. We came to evolve being. We must begin to show our love for each other and tune in to the things that really will make the human experience a well taken vacation. We must learn what unconditional love is, what reverence and sacredness is. Some of us have lost the meaning of sacred and minimized some of the most holy things in life. We have been destroying nature and killing our parent. It is time to stop the madness and get in touch with possibility. Peace is possible and the people that don't believe it will be pulled into it anyway regardless of whether they want to or not. I know these are not new concepts, but this is my way of sharing it and bringing to the world yet another reminder of what we all know on a very deep level. We are all pure love and the world will shift once we all start honoring, sharing and spreading the love to all people everywhere. No one excluded. Love is truly for us all, no matter what, no matter where, no matter who you are. You deserve it and once you start giving it and living it, your life will expand and you will open to the beauty, magnificence and grandeur of the experience of our existence.